My Little French Kitchen

Over 100 Recipes from the Mountains, Market Squares, and Shores of France

Rachel Khoo

Photographs by David Loftus and illustrations by Rachel Khoo

CHRONICLE BOOKS

SAN FRANCISCO

First published in the United States of America in 2014 by Chronicle Books LLC.
First published in the United Kingdom in 2013 by Michael Joseph, an imprint of Penguin Books, LTD.

Text and illustrations copyright © 2013 by Rachel Khoo.
Photographs copyright © 2013 by David Loftus.

Library of Congress Cataloging-in-Publication Data available.
ISBN 978-1-4521-3507-6

Manufactured in Italy

10 9 8 7 6 5 4 3 2 1

Chronicle Books LLC
680 Second Street
San Francisco, California 94107
www.chroniclebooks.com

Introduction

After the whirlwind months that followed the release of *The Little Paris Kitchen* book and television show, my life seemed to go back to normal. I was still living in the same apartment with my kitchenette composed of two gas burners and a mini oven, still no dishwasher in sight. I bought my grocery shopping from the same fruit and veg guy, visited the same baker, and traipsed to my butcher. Little had changed. Aside from my cheese lady's persistent jokey questioning, "Where are the cameras?" each time I picked up a hunk of fruity Comté, life went on in my little kitchen as before. But I could feel a growing rumble in my stomach, and it wasn't because I was craving a piece of French cheese and crusty baguette, my all-time favorite snack.

Just like when I moved from London to Paris eight years ago, I had an itchy yearning for new tastes and discoveries. I still loved Paris (I always will), but I felt I wanted to chart unknown territories in the country I had called home for almost a decade. It was time for me to pack up my cooking kit and discover what lay beyond the twenty arrondissements that piece Paris together.

Deciding where to go was easier said than done. When it comes to culinary culture and history, France is as rich and dense as my chocolate beret cake (see page 130). My friends asked, "How are you going to visit the whole of France and write about all the food? *Ce n'est pas possible!*" Most of them thought I had bitten off more than I could chew, and I can chew a lot! France has a gastronomic wealth that has been documented painstakingly by many other chefs and Francophile food writers throughout the centuries, from Marie-Antoine Carême and Auguste Escoffier to Elizabeth David and Jane Grigson.

This book took me on an adventure around France by train, plane, bus, car, and bike—at one point, I was even driving a minibus. Up winding roads and down dirt tracks, through howling wind, rain *comme les vaches pissent* (like cows peeing, as the French say), snow, hail . . . you name it, I braved every kind of weather. I was a woman on a mission to discover those recipes, now long forgotten and stuffed in the back of a drawer, made by regional French grandmas. But not just the old recipes; I was interested to see what France looked like today. How was the younger generation eating? Paris, being the capital, is a mecca for new concepts and trends, but I was impressed to see that a movement of young food producers can also be found all over the country, combining old traditions with their new ideas.

France's artisanal food scene, in common with other countries in the Western world, is fighting against the big food corporations. Although France has always prided itself on its strong culinary heritage, as I visited producers, farmers, and local shops it became evident that all is not as rosy as one might think. There are battles against environmental changes and government regulations, combined with the lack of a new generation to take over traditional roles and a sharp rise in production costs. But despite all these challenges, the passion and hard work that go into creating products to sell with pride shines through brightly in the end result.

After each of my voyages, I would return with my suitcase laden with random bits and bobs I had picked up, from edible souvenirs like special dried herbs and lavender honey to cheese paper wrappers or the odd funny looking spoon. In my little kitchen in Paris, the tasty trinkets would be turned into dishes to eat with friends and family. Each meal telling the story of my trip, allowing me to share my edible exploration and the complexities and oddities of each region's food culture.

My travels took me to many places all across this wonderful country, from Biarritz, the surfers' paradise, with its fiery Espelette pepper and Basque kisses, to the elegant chateaux and rickety but utterly charming oyster shacks in the Bordeaux region. I fell in love with the Christmas sparkle and spice of the Alsatian winter markets, and Brittany with its iconic lighthouses dotting the coast and its delicious giant blue lobsters. And I marveled at the almighty Lyon with its snowcapped mountains and warming dishes, which contrasted with the bright colors in the vegetable dishes of Provence that radiated summer heat.

And so this book is not about the whole of France—even a multivolume epic couldn't hope to do justice to that idea—but it is about the trips I made around French villages and towns; the people who welcomed me into their homes, farms, and food shops; and all the little culinary quirks that I stumbled upon. Each recipe is a postcard from my little kitchen to yours, savoring the flavors, smells, and textures that inspired me, and that I hope will inspire you too. *Bon voyage* on my little culinary tour of France! I hope you enjoy the trip.

Brittany

LA COQUILLE SAINT-JACQUES

LES MOULES

LE HOMARD BLEU

LA MANCHE

L'AGNEAU PRÉ SALÉ

LE PHARE

BREST

ST-MALO

MONT ST-MICHEL

LES CHAPEAUX BRETONS

LE SARRASIN

QUIMPER

DINAN

BRETAGNE

OCEAN ATLANTIQUE

NORMANDIE

LE CIDRE

RENNES

VANNES

LA FLEUR DE SEL

THON

JAM

LES CONSERVES

LES ALGUES

LES CRÊPES

LE BEURRE

LES GALETTES

LE TRICOT RAYÉ

LAIT RIBOT MALO

LE LAIT RIBOT

LES CARAMEL AU BEURRE SALÉ

BLUE-AND-WHITE STRIPES, BUTTERY DELIGHTS, AND COASTAL COOKING

Le crachin, as the Bretons refer to the so-called spitting rain, was almost constant when I visited the region in the early months of the year. The persistent drizzle wasn't the only thing that was like home: the lush green pastures, neatly trimmed hedges, and pretty stone country cottages reminded me of the verdant British landscape around where I grew up in Berkshire. It is easy to see how Brittany acquired the nickname "Little Britain."

Brittany is one of France's most iconic regions, being the home of many of the country's most popular foodstuffs, as well as the sartorial export of blue-and-white stripes. Butter, galettes, crêpes, caramel, *fleur de sel*, dairy and all its derivatives are entrenched in the food culture.

Thanks to this abundance of dairy and other such delights, Brittany is one of the best places in France to have breakfast. French breakfasts are often an afterthought, usually consisting of a cup of black coffee and a flaky croissant at best, and a toasted leftover baguette at worst. However, I enjoyed some exemplary homemade breakfasts during my stays at various B&Bs around the region, including homemade jams and breads as well as the thickest, creamiest homemade yogurt, which inspired my recipe on page 53. One of the most epic versions featured the legendary golden, caramelized *kouign-amann* (see page 42), Brittany's greatest pastry.

Now, crêpes and galettes were nothing new to me; Paris has a *crêperie* on every corner, and around the Montparnasse area there are plenty of Breton *crêperies*. However, what I found rather intriguing was what they filled their buckwheat pancakes with. Not the usual egg and cheese, but a grilled, quite spicy (for the French) sausage. Simply popped whole into the middle of each galette, then wrapped tightly to make a sort of galette hot dog. At the morning markets of Dinan and Rennes, this unlikely breakfast treat was de rigueur from the various food trucks sandwiched between produce sellers.

Markets are among Brittany's highlights. The *Marché des Lices* on Saturdays in the center of Rennes is probably one of the best I've been to in France. Unlike most Parisian markets, where the selection is excellent, but resellers (not farmers) operate most stands, in Rennes the producers themselves run the majority. Being in a coastal corner of France, the choice of seafood is out of this world. I have never seen such big lobsters, oysters in every size and shape possible, cockles, clams, razor clams, mussels, scallops, and fish fresh off the boat, glistening on ice.

More secrets were discovered on a trip to Saint-Malo, the beautiful town on the coast set within a medieval wall. Down a cobbled street I found the king of butter, Yves Bordier, with his renowned boutique and restaurant, complete with butter museum. Bretons love their butter, and Yves Bordier reigns supreme on the menus of the finest restaurants in France and abroad. His butter looks like little yellow bricks flecked with sea salt, seaweed, smoked salt, or even yuzu.

The rugged beauty of Brittany's coast is awe-inspiring. Lighthouses pop up on rocky cliffs with stretches of sandy beaches sandwiched in between. Cap Fréhel lies on such a cliff, with its majestic green-tipped beacon in a protected nature reserve. Small rocks jut out of the wet sand at low tide, revealing wild mussels and seaweed. The salt in the air has you licking your lips, stirring up an appetite for a picnic or some cooking on the beach.

Sea salt is big business in Brittany, but also a very time-consuming one. It is carefully harvested mainly around Guérande, the southwestern corner of Brittany where they produce the famous *fleur de sel*, a sea salt prized by chefs and food enthusiasts. Salt is harvested in the summer months, but requires meticulous attention throughout the year in preparation, as well as a great deal of savoir faire adapting to the whims of the weather at any time. Clay walls are built and maintained inside ponds for the salt water to be ushered though, and it is eventually raked into piles to dry. The *fleur de sel* are the delicate crystals that develop on the top of the water and they are pulled aside.

From the knob of butter that sizzles in the pan to the understated sprinkle of salt that brings an entire dish together, the gastronomy of Brittany may not have sophisticated Parisian glamour, but it is responsible for produce that is fundamental to dishes created in renowned restaurants around the world. From moist sea bass baked in a salt crust to buttermilk lamb to choux pastry lighthouses with butter caramel sauce (see pages 16, 30, and 46), the recipes in this chapter draw their inspiration from those little touches and apply them to dishes that can be cooked in any kitchen (whether home or Michelin-starred). I hope you fall for the food of Brittany as much as I did.

Huîtres grillées en persillade

OYSTERS GRILLED WITH PARSLEY CRUMBS

I love the purity of a just-shucked oyster, either as it comes or with a simple squeeze of lemon. But when they are in such abundance, as they are in Cancale and other parts of Brittany, you might as well experiment with different flavors. The crunchy texture of the breadcrumbs highlights the smoothness of the oyster flesh, providing a playful and delicious contrast.

Makes 12 oysters
Preparation time: 10 minutes
Cooking time: 10 minutes

2 tbsp butter

2 cloves of garlic, finely minced

4 tbsp/15 g white breadcrumbs
(made from stale bread)

4 tbsp/15 g finely chopped
flat-leaf parsley

12 oysters, shucked (see page 58)

Lemon wedges for serving

Heat a frying pan over medium heat. Add the butter and garlic. Once the butter is melted and the garlic slightly softened, add the breadcrumbs, stirring every so often until light golden, about 5 minutes. Place in a bowl and toss with the parsley.

Preheat the broiler to high. Remove any excess juices from your shucked oysters. Place the oysters on a tray that will hold them flat (madeleine or muffin pans work well) and broil for 2 to 3 minutes. Sprinkle the breadcrumb mixture over the oysters and serve immediately, passing the lemon wedges.

Une petite astuce—tip If you don't have a madeleine or muffin pan, make a bed out of rock salt on a baking sheet and nestle the oysters in it.

Faire en avance—get ahead The parsley breadcrumbs can be made in advance and stored in an airtight container for a couple of days.

Unshucked oysters will keep for about 2 days. Check with your fishmonger.

Court bouillon Breton

BRITTANY BOUILLON

Forget salty stock cubes and their powdered counterparts—in Brittany, packets of gourmet bouillon are de rigueur. Made using the locally available seaweed, this pantry staple essential takes on a new tang. Try adding this homemade bouillon to soups, sprinkling on salads, or popping into a stew for a taste of *Bretagne*.

Makes about 1 oz/30 g
Preparation time: 20 minutes
Cooking time: 3 to 4 hours
Resting time: overnight

2 carrots, peeled

2 sticks of celery (ideally with leaves)

2 leeks, trimmed and washed

10 mushrooms, brushed

1 clove of garlic

1 tsp coarse sea salt

½ cup/10 g dried seaweed

Preheat the oven to 225°F. Use a vegetable peeler to make thin ribbons of carrot. Finely slice the celery. Pull apart the layers of the leek, then cut into thin slices. Finely slice the mushrooms and garlic. Try to make all the vegetables an even thickness so that they take the same amount of time to cook.

Lay all the vegetables flat on parchment and arrange the celery leaves among the vegetables. Place the parchment directly on the oven rack and cook for 3 to 4 hours, or until the vegetables lose their moisture and crisp up. Turn off the heat and leave them to dry overnight in the oven with the door propped open slightly.

Pulse the dried vegetables with the salt and seaweed in a food processor until finely ground. Store in an airtight container in a cool dark place for up to 2 months.

Une petite astuce—tip Make your own bouillon "tea bags" for a quick cup of soup. Cut out six squares of muslin, each approximately 3 by 3 inches. Place 1 tbsp of the mixture in the center of each muslin square. Gather the corners together and twist the ends tightly. Use a length of thread to secure the bag in a tight knot; leave a long piece of thread for dunking. Repeat with the rest of the muslin squares. Store in an airtight container for up to 2 months.

Daurade en croûte de sel

HERBY SALT CRUST–BAKED BREAM

Baking in a salt crust is one of the most effective ways of cooking a whole fish. Not only is it dramatic to unveil the flesh from under a firm cast of salt at the dinner table, but the salt also traps all the moisture in the flesh while delicately seasoning it.

Serves 4
Preparation time: 10 minutes
Cooking time: 20 minutes

1 lemon, zested and cut into wedges

8 cups/1.5 kg coarse sea salt

2 whole sea bream or sea bass
(1 lb/450 g each), gutted and rinsed

1 bunch sorrel or flat-leaf parsley

2 egg whites

Steamed new potatoes, tossed in butter, for serving

Preheat the oven to 400°F. Line a baking sheet with parchment.

In a large bowl, combine the lemon zest with the salt. Stuff two lemon wedges into the cavity of each fish, along with two sorrel leaves. Chop up the rest of the sorrel and set aside 2 or 3 tbsp for garnish. Mix the rest into the lemony salt, then mix in the egg whites. Spread half of the salt mixture over the lined baking sheet. Lay the fish on top (with a few inches between them). Cover the fish with the rest of the salt and bake for 20 minutes.

Remove the fish from the oven and use a knife to crack the crust and gently peel off the salt. Serve the fish immediately with steamed new potatoes. Sprinkle the reserved sorrel over the top.

Une petite astuce—tip Make sure to use coarse sea salt as fine sea salt will dissolve in the egg white and won't form a solid crust.

Millefeuilles aux tomates et lentilles

TOMATO AND LENTIL MILLE-FEUILLE

You can't visit Brittany or Normandy and not eat a sweet crêpe or a savory galette (from which this mille-feuille is made). They are what choucroute is to the Alsatians; *pintxos* (see page 104) are to the Basques, and quenelles (see page 184) are to the Lyonnais. They are an integral part of the food culture and best enjoyed with a bottle of the locally produced cider.

Serves 6

Preparation time: 40 minutes
Resting time: 1 hour, or overnight
Cooking time: 40 minutes

1⅔ cups/200 g buckwheat flour

Salt

2½ cups cold water

Vegetable oil for frying

½ cup/100 g Puy or beluga lentils

1 large zucchini, finely chopped

2 red bell peppers, seeded and finely chopped

7 oz/200 g cherry tomatoes, finely chopped

1 red onion, finely chopped

1 tbsp olive oil, plus extra for drizzling

Freshly ground pepper

10½ oz/300 g tomatoes, assorted sizes and colors

1 tbsp lemon thyme

In a medium bowl, combine the flour and a pinch of salt. Make a well in the center and gradually mix in the water, adding just enough for the batter to have the consistency of cream. Don't overmix, as this will produce rubbery galettes. Refrigerate the batter for at least an hour, or overnight. Before using, whisk again and add more water if necessary to thin to a pouring consistency.

Heat a 6- to 8-inch nonstick crêpe pan or small frying pan over medium heat and brush with a little vegetable oil. Pour in a small ladleful of the batter and quickly swirl the pan so that the batter coats the base evenly. Cook for 1 to 2 minutes, loosen around the edge with a spatula, then flip it and cook for 1 minute more. Slide the galette out of the pan, then repeat to make 12 galettes, greasing the pan with a little oil each time. Stack the galettes with layers of paper towel or parchment between each one.

Bring 4 cups of salted water to a boil and cook the lentils until tender, about 20 minutes. Drain the lentils, cool, and combine with the zucchini, bell peppers, cherry tomatoes, onion, and olive oil. Season with salt and pepper.

Preheat the oven to 350°F. Line a 6- to 8-inch springform pan with parchment. Place one galette at the bottom of the pan. Spread with some of the lentil mixture, then top with another galette. Repeat until you have used up all the galettes (finishing with a galette).

Slice the assorted tomatoes and arrange on top of the galettes, overlapping slightly. Drizzle with a little olive oil and sprinkle with the thyme. Bake for 20 minutes, until warmed through, and serve.

Les sardines rapides au vinaigre

QUICK PICKLED SARDINES

Shiny silver sardines from Brittany are renowned in the Breton markets. Swimming against the strong tides of the Quiberon Peninsula, the fish develop a firmer flesh compared to their southern European cousins. As a means of preserving their abundant catches, the Quiberonnaise have a long-standing tradition of cooking these little fish and preserving them under a layer of salted butter. An industry grew out of this and you'll find many small factories preserving the local product in dinky tins. This kind of preservation *en boite* tastes best when it's had at least a couple of days for the flavors to develop. This recipe is quite the opposite: too long in the fridge and you'll be left with sardine mush on your hands, making it a perfect recipe for those who are impatient.

Serves 5 or 6 as a starter
Preparation time: 10 minutes
Resting time: 6 hours, or overnight

⅔ cup cider vinegar

⅔ cup white wine vinegar

½ cup/100 g sugar

2 tsp table salt

2 bay leaves

10 black peppercorns

2 juniper berries

20 fresh sardine fillets, boned

1 small cucumber, sliced into very thin rounds

1 small red onion, finely sliced

1 lemon, zested and cut into wedges

Buttered rye bread or Caraway and Apple Crackers (page 234)

In a medium saucepan, combine both vinegars, the sugar, salt, bay leaves, peppercorns, and juniper berries. Bring to a boil, stirring until the sugar dissolves. Remove from the heat and cool to room temperature.

Pour the brine into a shallow, nonmetallic dish. Add the sardine fillets (check for bones), cucumber, onion, and lemon zest. Make sure everything is submerged in the liquid. Cover the dish in plastic wrap and refrigerate for at least 6 hours, or overnight.

Serve on rye bread with wedges of lemon.

Les petites astuces—tips Ask your fishmonger to fillet your sardines for you.

Pickled sardines will turn mushy after about 24 hours.

Pâtes à la marinière au calvados

CLAM PASTA WITH CALVADOS CREAM

While in Brittany, I had the pleasure of meeting a dynamic young fellow, David Le Ruyet, who is on a one-man mission to make an impact on the local food scene. David grows his own wheat, mills it, and then makes pasta, which he sells throughout France and beyond. Due to the weather conditions of the region, David works with the local wheat flour (*blé tendre*) rather than the traditional durum wheat used in pasta making.

Serves 4
Preparation time: 15 minutes
Cooking time: 15 minutes

9 oz/250 g fettuccine, fusilli,
or conchiglie

1 onion, finely chopped

1 tbsp butter

⅔ cup calvados

5½ lb/2.5 kg clams or cockles, or a mix, scrubbed, broken ones discarded

4 tbsp crème fraîche

1 cup/145 g peas, in their pods

4 medium fresh sorrel leaves or a handful of parsley, finely chopped

½ lemon, zested and cut into wedges

Bring a large pot of salted water to a boil. Add the fettuccine and cook until al dente. Drain well.

Meanwhile, in a second large pot, cook the onion in the butter until soft and translucent. Add the calvados, followed by the clams. Cover and cook for 2 minutes. Stir, cover, and cook for 2 to 4 minutes more; the clams should open up once cooked. (If using cockles, cook them for just 2 minutes.) Strain the clams through a colander placed over a bowl to catch the liquid; discard any clams that remain closed.

Return the drained pasta to its pot and place over medium heat. Add 4 tbsp of the strained clam cooking liquid, the clams, onion, crème fraîche, peas, sorrel, and lemon zest. Toss to combine, then serve immediately with the lemon wedges.

Moules aux pommes et calvados

APPLE AND CALVADOS POTTED MUSSELS

The Breton coastline boasts a particularly pretty lighthouse painted a vibrant green. Along the spotless sandy beaches at the foot of this lighthouse are jagged gray rocks sticking out of the sand, and clinging to them are thousands of mussels. When I was there, a few locals were making the most of the bounty, picking them off the rocks and smuggling them into bags. Back in my Paris kitchen, I decided to combine mussels with some of the other products from Normandy and Brittany: butter and calvados.

Serves 4

Preparation time: 20 minutes
Cooking time: 20 minutes
Resting time: at least 1 hour
Equipment: four 6-oz glasses or ramekins

1 cup/200 g butter, softened

3½ tbsp calvados

2¼ lb/1 kg mussels, debearded, scrubbed, and rinsed in cold water

1 shallot, finely chopped

1 small tart apple, finely diced

Salt

Generous pinch of ground white pepper

2 tbsp finely chopped flat-leaf parsley

Crusty bread for serving

In a small saucepan over low heat, melt the butter. Set aside.

Pour the calvados into a large pot over high heat and, when it begins to steam, throw in the mussels and cover with the lid. Shake the pan from time to time. After 5 minutes all the mussels should have opened up. Cool slightly before removing them from their shells and setting to one side. Discard the empty shells and any mussels that are still closed.

Using a slotted spoon, remove the milk solids (the white foam on top) from the butter.

Add 2 tbsp of the clarified butter to a large frying pan set over medium to high heat. Add the shallot and apple and sauté until the shallot is translucent. Add all the mussels and gently warm through for a couple of minutes before removing from the heat. Taste for seasoning; add salt, if needed, and the white pepper, and then stir in the parsley.

Divide the mixture between the four ramekins and pour the remaining butter over the top. Leave to cool before refrigerating. The mussels taste best when they've had a little time for the flavors to develop; but if you really can't wait, simply chill until the butter has set to room temperature. Serve with the bread. Consume within 2 days.

Agneau au lait ribot avec sarrasin et salade d'herbe

BUTTERMILK LAMB WITH TOASTED BUCKWHEAT AND HERB SALAD

You might call fourth-generation specialist farmer Yannick Frain the ambassador of *mouton prés-salés*. His sheep (mostly black-faced Suffolk) live in the shadow of Mont Saint-Michel. This location not only provides an impressive backdrop, but when the tide is up during the full moon, the marshes are submerged in salt water. Grazing on this grass imparts a unique flavor to the meat.

Serves 4 to 6
Preparation time: 20 minutes
Resting time: overnight to 2 days
Cooking time: 4 hours

2½ lb/1.2 kg lean leg of lamb

¾ cup buttermilk

¾ cup water

Salt and freshly ground black pepper

2½ cups/400 g buckwheat groats

Large bunch of mint

Large bunch of flat-leaf parsley

1 lemon, juiced

4 tbsp olive oil

For the yogurt sauce

Zest and juice of ½ lemon

2½ cups/600 g plain yogurt

1 red onion, finely chopped

Pinch of sugar

Salt and freshly ground black pepper

Combine the lamb and buttermilk in a deep casserole dish or Dutch oven. Cover tightly. Refrigerate to marinate for 24 to 48 hours.

Preheat the oven to 325°F. Add the water to the lamb and buttermilk, season with plenty of salt and pepper, and bake for 3½ hours, basting every hour or so with the cooking liquid. Remove from the oven and cover with lightly greased foil to rest for 10 minutes.

Meanwhile, place a large saucepan over medium heat. Add the buckwheat and dry-toast for about 5 minutes, until it is golden brown and has a nutty fragrance. Remove from the heat and cool to room temperature. Tear the mint and parsley leaves into the buckwheat and add a pinch of salt, the lemon juice, and oil. Toss to combine, then set aside.

To make the yogurt sauce: Mix the lemon zest and juice with the yogurt, onion, and sugar. Season with salt and pepper.

Slice the meat and serve on top of the buckwheat with the yogurt sauce drizzled over.

Sablés aux fromage et tomates

CHEESE AND TOMATO BUTTERY BISCUITS

I have a confession to make: I have a soft spot for those tiny pizza-flavored crackers you find in France. I was enjoying an aperitif in Brittany when I was offered a small plate of them, which I quickly polished off and began considering a home-baked version. A *sablé* (meaning "sandy") is quite simply a very buttery cookie, and shops selling different versions of the *sablé Breton* are as common as *crêperies* in the region. They are a poshed-up yet easy-to-make version of the tiny pizza aperitif crackers you can buy at the supermarket.

Makes 50 biscuits
Preparation time: 20 minutes
Resting time: 30 minutes
Cooking time: 10 minutes

1¼ cups/150 g all-purpose flour

½ cup plus 1 tbsp/125 g cold butter, cut into small cubes

4½ oz/125 g finely grated mature Tomme or other strongly flavored hard cheese

7 oz/200 g cherry tomatoes, sliced

1 to 2 tbsp fresh oregano

In a large bowl, combine the flour, butter, and cheese. Rub the butter and cheese into the flour with your fingertips until you have a sandy texture, then start squashing it together to make it a ball. Wrap the ball of dough in plastic wrap and then roll it into a sausage shape, about 1¼ inches in diameter. Refrigerate for at least 30 minutes to relax the dough.

Preheat the oven to 350°F. Line a baking sheet with parchment.

Remove the dough from the refrigerator, peel off the plastic, and slice the dough into thin rounds. Place the rounds on the lined baking sheet, topping each one with a slice of tomato and a pinch of oregano. Bake for 10 minutes, or until golden on the bottom. Cool on a rack before serving. These keep, in an airtight container, for up to 2 days.

Les petites astuces—tips Be careful, as the *sablés* will be very fragile when they come out of the oven.

The tomatoes can be replaced with slices of olives or little pieces of anchovy.

Faire en avance—get ahead The dough can be frozen. Simply slice it and bake from frozen, adding a few minutes to the baking time.

Soupe de homard, lait ribot et fenouil

LOBSTER, FENNEL, AND BUTTERMILK SOUP

The lobsters I spotted at the Saturday morning market in Rennes looked more like the deep-sea monsters you imagine as a kid. I have never seen lobsters quite so big and in such abundance. I can only imagine that the Bretons feel that these beautiful lobsters are simply too good to be sent away from their region. Fair play, I say; if I were a local I would agree!

Serves 4
Preparation time: 20 minutes
Cooking time: 1¼ hours

1 cooked lobster (about 2¼ lb/1 kg) or 4 lobster tails

1 head of fennel

2 lemons, zested

2 tbsp butter

1 onion, roughly chopped

2 bay leaves

10 black peppercorns

1 cup white wine

4 cups water

1 cup buttermilk

Salt

Lobster roe for garnish (optional)

Carefully remove the lobster meat from the shell or ask your fishmonger to cut it in half to make it easier. Place the meat in a bowl, cover with plastic wrap, and refrigerate until needed.

Cut the fennel in half lengthwise. Chop one half roughly and set aside to use in the stock. Finely slice the other half, discarding the tough stem. Save the green fronds for garnish. Juice half a lemon over the sliced fennel and refrigerate.

Place a large saucepan over medium heat and add the butter, chopped fennel, onion, bay leaves, the zest from 1 lemon, the lobster shells, and the peppercorns. Cook, stirring, until the onion is translucent. Add the wine, increase the heat to high, and simmer for 2 minutes. Add the water, cover, and simmer gently for 30 minutes. Do not allow it to boil.

Place a fine-mesh sieve over a large bowl. Pour the stock through the sieve, pressing to get the most out of the tasty solids. Discard the solids. Return the strained stock to the pot and bring to a simmer. Simmer for 30 minutes, uncovered.

Remove the lobster from the refrigerator 30 minutes before serving. Add the buttermilk to the stock with a squeeze of lemon; the buttermilk will solidify into clusters. Season with salt.

Divide the lobster meat between four serving bowls, pour the stock over the top, and add the finely sliced fennel, the remaining zest, the fennel fronds, and the lobster roe, if desired. Serve immediately.

Paupiette au poulet, chataigne et pomme avec salade de chou-rave

ROASTED CHICKEN PARCELS WITH KOHLRABI SLAW

Apple orchards are a fixture of the agricultural landscape of Brittany and Normandy, so it is no surprise that the drink of choice is cider and, for those wanting to put a little hair on their chest, calvados. I tasted a surprising cider from Sacha Crommar, who is part of a local group of producers experimenting with and refining traditional techniques in the region. To make his Cidre Chataigne, the pressed juice is fermented with chestnuts, adding an earthy complexity. That combination of tastes inspired this dish; perfect for a lazy Sunday lunch and easily prepared in advance—the chicken can be stuffed and kept in the fridge, covered, for up to 48 hours.

Serves 4

Preparation time: 30 minutes
Cooking time: 45 minutes

4 large boneless chicken thighs, skin on

Salt and freshly ground black pepper

3 shallots

1 small apple, finely diced

1 cup/100 g shelled walnuts, finely chopped

¾ cup/120 g cooked and peeled chestnuts, crushed into crumbs

8 to 12 slices of cooked bacon

1¼ cups dry cider

For the slaw

1 kohlrabi or celeriac, peeled and grated

½ apple, unpeeled, grated

Squeeze of lemon juice

2 tbsp olive oil

Salt

Preheat the oven to 400°F. Season the chicken thighs on both sides with salt and pepper. Spread out each thigh, skin-side down. Chop half a shallot very finely and mix it with the apple, walnuts, and chestnuts. Divide the stuffing among the middles of the thighs, then fold over the sides of the meat so it covers the stuffing and joins in the middle. Secure with a toothpick through each end and one through the middle.

Wrap 2 or 3 slices of bacon around the sides, securing them with a toothpick. Take a length of butcher's string and wrap up the chicken parcel as pictured on the facing page.

Chop the rest of the shallots roughly and scatter in a baking dish. Arrange the chicken thighs on top and pour in the cider. Bake for 45 minutes or until the juices run clear when the thigh is tested.

Just before serving, make the slaw: Mix together the kohlrabi and apple. Drizzle with the lemon juice and oil and season with salt.

Remove the toothpicks from the chicken and serve atop the slaw. Drizzle some of the remaining pan juices over the top.

Une petite astuce—tip Don't make the slaw too far in advance, as the apple will brown.

Paris-Brest salé

SAVORY PARIS-BREST

Legend has it that the original Paris-Brest, now a classic among French pastries, was created by *chef pâtissier* Louis Durand in 1910 to celebrate the famous Paris-Brest bicycle race. The traditional version is a simple choux pastry ring (or bicycle tire, as the shape represents) filled with a voluptuous praline cream. In homage to my trip from Paris to Brest, I took inspiration from one of my favorite Parisian ingredients to transform this classic pastry into a savory delight. Instead of praline cream, this Paris-Brest is filled with Brie de Meaux, some delicious crunchy apples, and a little fresh spinach. A zingy mustard mousse ties everything together.

Makes 6 sandwiches

Preparation time: 30 minutes
Cooking time: 20 to 25 minutes
Equipment: a piping bag with a ⅜-inch nozzle

1 recipe Choux Pastry Dough (page 274)

Confectioners' sugar for dusting

6 tbsp/50 g chopped hazelnuts

For the mustard mousse

¼ cup/50 g heavy cream

1 tbsp wholegrain mustard

1 egg white

5½ oz/150 g Brie de Meaux (or other Brie), mature Comté, or Cheddar, finely sliced

2 small apples, cored and finely sliced

1 bunch baby spinach, leaves only

Scrape the choux dough into the piping bag. Line several baking sheets with parchment, dotting a little of the pastry dough in each corner to help the paper stick.

Preheat the oven to 350°F. Use a 4-inch plate to draw six circles on the parchment. Pipe a ring of the choux pastry just inside one of the lines. Pipe a second ring tightly inside the first ring, so they are touching. Pipe a third ring on top of the two. Dust with confectioners' sugar and sprinkle 1 tbsp of the hazelnuts over the top. Repeat with the other circle outlines. Bake for 20 to 25 minutes, or until golden brown. Remove from the oven to a baking rack to cool.

To make the mustard mousse: Whip the cream to soft peaks and then stir in the mustard. In a clean, grease-free glass or metal bowl, whip the egg whites until they form firm peaks. Fold the egg whites into the cream mixture.

Slice each ring in half horizontally. Lay slices of cheese on the bases, followed by slices of apple and the spinach leaves. Pipe or spoon little dollops of the mustard mousse on top of the spinach and replace the top of the choux pastry ring. Serve immediately.

Faire en avance—get ahead The choux pastry rings can be made 1 day in advance. Place on a baking sheet and cook in a 325°F oven for 10 minutes to crisp.

Les kouignettes aux groseilles

BUTTERY RED CURRANT PASTRIES

Kouignettes are mini versions of the famous Brittany pastry *kouign-amann*. It took at least three days of pointing at the cake in pâtisseries before I got my head around the pronunciation (the literal translation from Breton is "butter cake"). The simplest way to think of it is "queen" plus "am-an." Or in the case of my miniature versions, "queen" plus "et."

The traditional cake is not much more than a simple combination of butter and sugar, layered in the same way as puff pastry, but between a yeasted dough. You can tell a good *kouign-amman* just by looking at it (beware of pale imitations masquerading as the real thing); it should have a crunchy, deep caramel–colored shell, a sign it has been baked long and hot enough to make the pastry crisp and the sugar caramelized.

This recipe takes some understanding. Read the instructions through a couple of times if you're embarking on this for the first time, and have a look at the photos on page 44.

Makes 12 pastries

Preparation time: 1 hour

Resting time: 3 hours, or overnight

Cooking time: 30 minutes

Equipment: a rolling pin; 12-cup muffin pan

2 cups/260 g all-purpose flour

1 tsp instant yeast

1 tsp salt

¾ cup warm water

¾ cup plus 2 tbsp/200 g butter, frozen for 30 minutes

¾ cup/150 g sugar

2 handfuls of red currants, black currants, or lingonberries, frozen or fresh, stemmed

In a medium bowl, mix together the flour, yeast, and salt. Add the water and continue to mix until it forms a ball (if the dough is very dry add 1 tbsp water). Remove the dough from the bowl and knead for at least 10 minutes or until smooth. Place the dough back in the bowl, cover with plastic wrap, and leave in a warm place for 1 hour.

Cut the butter into very thin slices (roughly ¹⁄₁₆ inch thick). Refrigerate until needed.

Dust the work surface lightly with flour. Roll out the dough to a rectangle roughly 12 by 16 inches, with the short side facing you. Place the butter slices in the middle of the dough; they can overlap slightly. The butter should cover about half of the dough, leaving a quarter of the dough all the way around like a frame.

Fold the top and bottom edges of the dough over the butter to meet in the middle, like you're folding a letter. Take the rolling pin and press down gently all over the dough. Repeat folding and pressing one more time.

Fold the top half of the dough over the bottom half and turn the pastry so that you have the seam on the left (like a book). Roll out the dough again to a rectangle about 12 by 16 inches, with the short side facing you. Fold the bottom edge over to the middle, and fold the top down to meet it in the middle. Then fold the top half over the bottom half once more (this process is called a roll and fold). Wrap the dough tightly in plastic wrap (it will expand) and leave it to rest in the fridge for at least 2 hours, or preferably overnight.

Butter the muffin pan and leave in the fridge until needed.

When the dough has rested, put a baking sheet in the oven and preheat to 400°F. Sprinkle your work surface liberally with some of the sugar. Place the dough on top of the sugar (with the seam on the left) and sprinkle the dough with more sugar. Roll out the dough to a large rectangle about 12 by 16 inches, with the long side facing you. Add more sugar to the work surface if the dough begins to stick. Sprinkle the rest of the sugar on top of the pastry and scatter the berries on top. Roll up the dough tightly and cut into 12 equal slices. Place each *kouignette* in the muffin pan, put the muffin pan on the preheated baking sheet, and bake for 25 minutes, or until the *kouignettes* are a deep golden brown. Remove the *kouignettes* from the oven and leave to cool for 5 minutes before removing them from the pan. (Do not leave to cool completely in the pan or they will get stuck.) Cool completely and serve; these will not keep.

Une petite astuce—tip Cold hands and a cool kitchen will make this dough easier to handle. Run your hands under cold water before handling the pastry. If you have a metal, marble, or laminate work surface, place a large tray filled with ice cubes on the work surface for 30 minutes before adding the butter to the dough.

Faire en avance—get ahead You can freeze the *kouignettes* before baking. Defrost in the refrigerator for 8 hours before putting in the oven.

Phares au caramel, gingembre et framboise

CARAMEL, GINGER, AND RASPBERRY LIGHTHOUSES

Lighthouses are a quintessential sight along the Breton coast, as the waters around these ways are dangerous to navigate, with jagged rocks cropping up from nowhere. These iconic beacons of light have become a symbol of Brittany and can be spotted not only along the coast, but also in the many souvenir shops alongside the famous striped tops. When it comes to ornamental souvenirs I'm not too fussy, but edible ones? That's a whole different matter.

Serves 4

Preparation time: 40 minutes
Cooking time: 40 minutes
Resting time: 1 hour
Equipment: a piping bag with a ⅓-inch nozzle; 4 bamboo skewers

½ recipe Choux Pastry Dough (page 274)

Confectioners' sugar for dusting

For the ginger cream

6 egg yolks

6 tbsp/80 g sugar

5 tbsp/40 g cornstarch

1 to 2 tsp ground ginger

2 cups whole milk

20 raspberries

1 recipe Salted Butter Caramel (page 48)

Scrape the dough into the piping bag. Line two baking sheets with parchment, dotting a little of the dough in each corner to help the paper stick.

Preheat the oven to 350°F. Hold the piping bag at a 90-degree angle about ¼ inch from the lined baking sheet. Keep the nozzle upright and pipe four small walnut-size balls of dough, leaving a 1-inch gap between each one (they should be about 1 inch wide). Then pipe four slightly larger balls of dough on the same baking sheet. If any of the balls have little points, dip your finger in some water and gently pat the points down; otherwise they will burn in the oven.

On the second baking sheet, pipe four balls of dough that are a little bigger than the previous ones, and then pipe another four balls of dough, again, slightly bigger than the last set. These final balls should be about 1½ inches wide.

Dust with confectioners' sugar, then bake. After 20 minutes, remove the baking sheet with the smaller buns, and after another 10 minutes remove the second sheet. Set on baking racks to cool.

While the buns are baking, make the ginger cream: Whisk the egg yolks with the sugar until light and thick, then whisk in the cornstarch. Add the ginger to the milk in a small saucepan. Bring the milk to a boil and then turn off the heat. Pour the milk in a slow stream over the egg mixture, whisking vigorously.

Pour the mixture into a clean saucepan, place over medium heat, and whisk continuously. Scrape the sides and the bottom of the pan, otherwise the mixture will burn. The cream will start to thicken and bubble; immediately remove from the heat.

Line a shallow rimmed baking sheet with plastic wrap and pour in the mixture. Cover, pressing the plastic wrap on the surface of the cream, and refrigerate for at least 1 hour. When ready to use, beat with a whisk until smooth and pour into a piping bag.

Cut a small slit in the bottom of a choux bun. Hold it between your thumb and index finger with the slit facing up and squeeze gently so it opens. Push in a raspberry, then fill with the pastry cream. Repeat with all the buns.

Stack four choux buns on top of each other with the largest at the bottom and the smallest at the top. Use some caramel to stick them together. Pierce a bamboo skewer through the middle to keep the lighthouse upright while assembling the others.

Just before serving, remove the skewers. Pour more caramel over the top and top with a raspberry. I like to add a flag for the true lighthouse effect.

Caramel au beurre salé

SALTED BUTTER CARAMEL

It was only a matter of time before somebody in Brittany discovered that combining the region's staples of butter and cream with sugar and a pinch of salt, and then cooking it, could make something so utterly delicious. That hit of salt in Breton caramel turns a quite plain caramel into something very special. And the caramel is taken a shade darker than usual to create a slightly bitter note, which balances out the sugary sweetness. I love adding a spoonful to my morning yogurt.

Makes ¾ cup/250 g
Preparation time: 5 minutes
Cooking time: 15 minutes
Equipment: a kitchen thermometer

¾ cup/150 g sugar

7 tbsp heavy cream

2 tbsp runny honey

3 tbsp/40 g butter

½ tsp salt

Add half the sugar to a clean saucepan with 2 tbsp water. Place over medium-high heat and let the sugar dissolve. Do not stir; instead, gently swirl the saucepan.

Once the caramel has turned a dark reddish-brown, remove the pan from the heat and add the cream, honey, butter, and salt. Be careful not to stand over the pan as you do so, as the caramel will steam and bubble. Give the pan a good swirl and then return it to medium heat. Cook for 3 to 4 minutes, or until it reaches 235°F.

Remove the pan from the heat and let cool for a couple of minutes before pouring the caramel into a glass jar. The caramel will keep for a couple of months in the fridge; reheat and add a little water to thin it out.

To make soft-set caramels
Continue to cook the caramel over medium heat until it reaches 260°F. Pour the caramel into a small parchment-lined baking dish or rimmed baking sheet. Set for at least 1 hour before using a knife dipped in boiling water to cut into squares or bars.

Une petite astuce—tip For spiced caramel, add 1 tsp cinnamon and ½ tsp ground ginger; for a zingy touch, add the zest of 1 orange and 1 lemon; for a chocolaty finish, stir in 3 tbsp cocoa nibs.

Tartelettes Far Breton

PRUNE AND CUSTARD TARTLETS

Far Bretons are as ubiquitous as *phares Bretonnes* in Brittany (the same pronunciation, but definitely not to be confused with the lighthouses). The *far Breton* is a dense flan, similar to Limousin's clafoutis but studded with prunes, which takes its name from the Latin word for wheat. It was originally an economical dessert, simply sweetened with dried fruits. I love a slice of flan but I prefer mine to have a crisp caramelized crust to contrast with the soft center, like these bite-size morsels.

Makes 12
Preparation time: 30 minutes
Cooking time: 35 minutes
Equipment: a 12-cup muffin pan

8 tbsp sugar

12 oz/350 g puff pastry

12 soft, ready-to-eat pitted prunes

1¼ cups crème fraîche

2 eggs, plus 1 egg yolk

Pinch of salt

Butter the muffin pan. Dust the work surface with 2 tbsp of the sugar and roll out the puff pastry to a large rectangle about 16 by 12 inches, with the long side facing you. Dust with another 2 tbsp sugar and gently roll with a rolling pin to press in the sugar.

Roll up the pastry tightly and cut into twelve equal slices. Place each slice, cut-side up, in the muffin pan. Using your thumb, push the pastry outward and upward to evenly coat the inside of each cup, until it reaches the top.

Preheat the oven to 375°F. Place a prune in each tartlet. Whisk together the crème fraîche, remaining sugar, eggs, egg yolk, and salt. Fill each tartlet to ⅛ inch from the top. Bake for 35 minutes, or until the pastry is golden. Immediately remove the tartlets from the pan and place on a wire rack to cool. The tartlets can be refrigerated for up to 2 days, wrapped tightly.

Une petite astuce—tip The prunes can be replaced with other soft fruit such as apricots, dried apples, raspberries, or cherries—or you can simply leave them out for a plain version.

Yaourts aux coulis de framboise

RASPBERRY RIPPLE YOGURT

After Germany, the French are the biggest consumers of yogurt in Europe; the vast selection in the supermarket gives that away. And it's not just plain yogurt or fruit-flavored varieties but also yogurts made from goat's and sheep's milk. Yogurt isn't something you'd immediately think of making at home, as many people think you need a machine to achieve the right results. Determined to prove this was not the case (there is no more room in my little Paris kitchen for cookbooks, so a yogurt machine is out of the question), I set about testing out some recipes using my tiny oven. *Et voilá!*

Makes 4 to 6 small pots

Preparation time: 10 minutes

Resting time: 7 hours

Cooking time: 3 hours

Equipment: four to six 6-oz glass yogurt pots or ramekins; a kitchen thermometer (optional)

1¾ cups/300 g frozen raspberries

3 tbsp sugar

½ a vanilla pod, split lengthwise and seeds scraped out, or ¼ tsp freshly grated tonka bean

2 cups whole milk

½ cup/70 g powdered milk

5 tbsp/70 g organic full-fat plain "live" yogurt

2 tbsp crème fraîche

Place the raspberries, sugar, and vanilla seeds in a small saucepan. Place the saucepan over medium heat, stirring occasionally. Once the mixture has come to a boil, remove from the heat. Use an immersion blender to break up the raspberries and seeds (pass it through a sieve if you prefer a seed-free version). Divide the raspberry mixture between the yogurt pots and refrigerate until needed.

Place the milk and powdered milk in a small saucepan over medium heat until just simmering; 180°F on the kitchen thermometer. Remove from the heat and cool until you can comfortably dip your finger in the milk. Whisk in the yogurt and crème fraîche, making sure the yogurt completely blends into the milk. Carefully ladle the mixture into the yogurt pots.

Place the pots in a 125°F oven and leave for 3 hours without opening the door. Turn off the oven and leave for another 6 hours. Chill in the fridge for at least 1 hour before eating. The yogurt will keep in the fridge for up to 1 week.

Une petite astuce—tip Use an oven thermometer to accurately test the temperature of your oven. If the oven is too hot, the bacteria will be killed off.

Galette des rois

KING'S CAKE

This has to be one of my favorite French traditions. In France, the post-Christmas period is the time to celebrate Epiphany on January 6 with a rich frangipane galette. Captured in the galette is what they call the *fève*, which was originally a dried fava bean. These days a fancier little porcelain figurine is used, and whoever is lucky enough to land on the slice that contains it—without breaking a tooth—gets the honor of wearing a gold paper crown. Normally the galette is more like a pie, with the puff pastry encasing the almond cream, but I prefer to substitute hazelnuts for the almonds and cover mine with a layer of apples for a bit of a sharp contrast.

Serves 6 to 8

Preparation time: 30 minutes

Resting time: 30 minutes

Cooking time: 45 minutes

Equipment: a 7-inch springform cake pan, depth 3 inches; tiny ceramic figurine or clean penny; gold paper crown

12 oz/350 g puff pastry

1½ cups/150 g shelled blanched hazelnuts

6 tbsp/75 g sugar

Pinch of salt

7 tbsp/100 g very soft butter

1 egg

1 apple, unpeeled, cored and finely sliced

Line the bottom of the springform pan with parchment and grease the sides. Cut the puff pastry in half and roll out one half to fit the base of the pan, trimming away any excess. Roll out the other half to a rectangle, 6 by 14 inches, and cut it in half lengthwise.

Line the sides of the pan with one of the pastry strips, allowing a little overlap where the base meets the side. Use your fingertip to press down the overlap to make sure the pastry seals. Push the second half around the bottom of the pan where the sides and base join, allowing a little overlap.

Using a sharp knife, cut out triangles from the side to create a crown shape. (Make sure to leave a band at least 1½ inches high around the base or the hazelnut cream will spill out.) Refrigerate for 30 minutes.

Toast the hazelnuts in a dry pan until golden. Cool slightly before grinding to a fine powder. Beat together the sugar, hazelnuts, salt, and butter until smooth, then incorporate the egg. Spread the mixture evenly over the base of the pastry. Hide the small ceramic figurine in the pastry cream and cover with the sliced apple.

Place a baking sheet in the oven and preheat to 400°F. Put the cake in the oven on the hot baking sheet and lower the temperature to 350°F. Bake for 45 minutes, or until golden brown. If the pastry browns too quickly, cover with some foil. Serve warm. This cake will keep, lightly covered, for 1 day.

Bordeaux

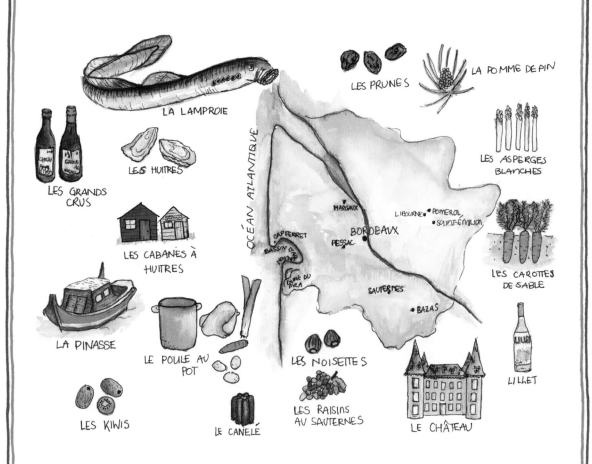

LA LAMPROIE

LES PRUNES

LA POMME DE PIN

LES GRANDS CRUS

LES HUITRES

LES ASPERGES BLANCHES

OCÉAN ATLANTIQUE

LES CABANES À HUITRES

CAP FERRET

BASSIN D'ARCACHON

DUNE DU PYLA

MARGAUX

LIBOURNE • POMEROL
• SAINT-ÉMILION

BORDEAUX

PESSAC

SAUTERNES

BAZAS

LES CAROTTES DE SABLE

LA PINASSE

LE POULE AU POT

LES NOISETTES

LILLET

LES KIWIS

LE CANELÉ

LES RAISINS AU SAUTERNES

LE CHÂTEAU

ELEGANT CHATEAUX, CHICKEN IN POTS, AND RICKETY OYSTER SHACKS

The majestic city of Bordeaux sits on the Garonne, a riverfront once lined with factories pumping out pollution. For many years, Bordeaux's bourgeois limestone buildings were coated with a thick layer of soot, developed over decades, even centuries, from the dirty emissions expelled by regional big industries. In the mid-'90s, *La Belle Endormie*, "the sleeping beauty" (Bordeaux's nickname), was awakened from its deep slumber with a rejuvenating program that saw the buildings scrubbed clean and the unused warehouses and factories along the river refurbished into smart new offices and apartments. A shiny new tram now glides effortlessly through the streets.

When I arrived in Bordeaux, there was little evidence of these historically black facades; quite the contrary, everything was gleaming white. Nosing along the cobbled streets of this vibrant town, it felt rather like a mini Paris with its grand symmetrical houses, fountains, and polished sculptures. *La Port de la Lune,* once an active industrial harbor, is now home to chic cafés, joggers, and open-air food markets. Prosperity, mainly generated by Bordeaux's most famous export, wine, is everywhere to behold and proudly so.

As a trained pastry chef, I had something more on my agenda than simply glugging a good glass of Chateau Margaux. *Canelé*, little caramelized cakes with a gooey custardy center, are a local specialty. In search of perfection, I tried endless pastry shops, even a dedicated *canelé* shop, but none compared to Alain Guignard's creations at his pâtisserie in Arcachon, a pretty seaside town southwest of Bordeaux; I had to re-create them in my own kitchen (see page 98).

Cap Ferret is the southwest's answer to St. Tropez. It is more laid-back, nestled in the Arcachon Bay. Walking along the beach on a clear day you can spot small fishing boats bopping about, big poles jutting out of the water with oyster cages tied to them, and plenty of colorful little fisherman's shacks and wooden beach houses lining the coast. This is prime oyster territory, and often the oysters don't make it farther than Bordeaux, as they're so prized by the locals.

Gazing out across the bay, you'll see a wide expanse of golden sand, the Dune of Pyla. From a distance its size is deceptive, but this sand dune is actually the tallest in Europe, and it's quite a trek to the top. It certainly felt like the sand extended for miles, like the Sahara of France.

Heading back inland you will discover a dozen chateaux, if not more, with rows and rows of vines. Bordeaux is one of France's most productive wine regions, home to the most expensive reds in the world. But the area wasn't known internationally for its wines until Henry Platagenet, who eventually became King Henry II of England, married Eleanor of Aquitaine in the twelfth century, making the Aquitaine territory English. He exported a large amount of Bordeaux claret in exchange for other goods, and spread the wine and its reputation throughout the world. Standing up with the great reds of Margaux, Saint-Émilion, and Pomerol, sweet Sauternes hold a lot of clout too. You'll spot delis selling prunes, raisins, and other dried fruit that have been soaked in this perfumed sweet wine, sometimes then covered in chocolate, making for delightful little nibbles.

I started to feel that there was a bit of a class system going on with the region's gastronomy. Wine was labeled *Premier Cru*, *Grand Cru Classé*, or *Vin de Table*, and oysters were graded 0 to 5, with the smaller number signifying the bigger oyster, and asparagus was sold by its thickness. But while the gastronomy seemed a little elitist, the cobbled streets of Bordeaux certainly didn't. There was a vibrant mix of food from all over the world alongside a handful of classic French eateries. Bordeaux has a big university, and, after speaking to a young Bordelais chef and restaurant owner, Aurélien Crosato, I learned that the majority of students are looking for a meal that fills you up without emptying your wallet, rather than a gourmet experience.

The wine flows generously in Bordeaux, at mealtimes and in the kitchen preparations. Whether you're trying out my quick Red Wine Roast Chicken (page 76) or the sweet seasoning of Sauternes in my crispy duck wraps (see page 80), wine proves to be a handy and delicious kitchen condiment. I can also recommend a glass of Saint-Émilion to enjoy while cooking, because it hits the spot perfectly when winding down after a long day. Just leave the knife skills to someone else.

Huîtres avec un bouillon Bordelais

OYSTERS IN A BORDELAIS BOUILLON

Little oyster shacks dot Arcachon Bay, which is just under an hour's drive west of Bordeaux. Along the coastal route are the so-called *villages ostréicoles*, which, in a nutshell, are like mini Disney Worlds for oyster lovers. One particularly picturesque example is that of the Village de l'Herbe, where rickety seafood shacks spill onto the beach and serve a dozen oysters with a glass of Tariquet for just a few euros.

Traditionally, oysters are simply shucked and served with a squeeze of lemon, but I'm combining them with another typical taste of the region: a hefty Bordeaux red from the nearby Médoc. A deep, rich bouillon is made using the red wine, which is then poured over the oysters to cook them quickly and give them a more meaty texture.

Makes 12 oysters
Preparation time: 15 minutes
Cooking time: 30 minutes

2 tbsp butter

2 shallots, finely sliced

⅔ cup red Bordeaux wine
(or another hearty red wine)

2 cups hot beef stock

Pinch of salt

2 tbsp red wine vinegar

12 oysters

Coarse sea salt

1 tbsp finely chopped chives

Melt the butter in a nonstick saucepan over medium heat and fry the shallots until golden and caramelized. Add the wine, bring to a boil, and boil for 10 minutes. Add the beef stock and salt and boil vigorously for 5 minutes. Turn off the heat and stir in the vinegar. Taste for seasoning.

Meanwhile, open the oysters. Use a special oyster knife (shucker) that has a guard and a dull blade with a pointed tip. Don't use an ordinary knife. First, wash and scrub the oysters under cold running water. Using a folded tea towel to protect your hand, place the oyster with its round bottom on a cutting board. Dig the tip of the shucker into the hinge (the pointy end of the oyster) and wiggle the blade along the hinge in order to loosen it. Twist the blade to open the shell a little. Keep the knife flush with the top shell and slide it along to separate the two shells and sever the muscle in the top half. Lift off the top shell and remove any broken pieces from the oyster flesh. If the oyster smells fishy or "off," discard it. Freshly shucked oysters should smell of the sea in a clean and fresh way.

Carefully detach the muscle from the bottom shell with the tip of the knife and drain away any remaining juices from the oyster. Rest the oysters on a bed of sea salt. Ladle the boiling bouillon over them, sprinkle with the chives, and serve immediately.

Tartare de crabe et kiwi

CRAB AND KIWI TARTARE

I always think of the kiwi as an exotic fruit, with its fuzzy brown outside concealing a bright green, juicy center. But, as I traveled around the region, they kept popping up at food markets and in fruit bowls at breakfast, and I was pleasantly surprised to find out that they have been grown in the Landes region, just south of Bordeaux, since the 1960s. Not only does their vibrant color and zing bring a welcome freshness to the bleak winter fruit selection (the harvest takes place in October and November, making January the best month for eating them), but also their sweet acidity marries beautifully with the local seafood. Chopped up and tossed with some sweet crabmeat and crunchy cucumber, they make a fine little starter.

Serves 4 as a starter
Preparation time: 20 minutes

½ lime, zested

3 oz/80 g chilled crabmeat

2 ripe kiwis, peeled and cut into small cubes

1 shallot, finely chopped

One 4-inch piece of cucumber, seeded and cut into small cubes

Salt (optional)

4 slices of bread

1 tbsp unsalted soft butter

Add ½ tsp of the lime zest to a bowl, then break the crabmeat into the bowl. Add the kiwis, shallot, and cucumber. Squeeze in the juice from the lime half and toss to coat. Taste for seasoning and add salt, if needed.

Toast the bread and cut it into triangles. Spread the bread with the butter and arrange on a plate next to a bowl of the crab tartare. Eat immediately.

Une petite astuce—tip For an especially pretty starter, use a 3-inch biscuit cutter to cut out four circles from the toast. Spread with the butter, then place the biscuit cutter on top and fill with the crab tartare to create neat mounds.

Arcachon Bay

POINTES 9
COURTES 8.50
LONGUES 8
12.16 .... 7.50
.... 7.
TÊTES VERTES ....
.... 5
FINES balais ....

ASPERGES

Asperges blanches habillées

WHITE ASPARAGUS IN BLANKETS

When I visit producers, I always like to find out how they like to eat what they produce. Usually it's the simplest way of cooking: a quick blanch, a lick of flame on the barbecue, or a speedy steam. While visiting the Perroto family's asparagus farm, I found that Monsieur preferred his white asparagus blanched and served with a knob of butter and a sprinkle of salt, whereas Madame whisked up a quick asparagus omelette with a splash of white wine and served it with some Bayonne ham. I tasted white spears fresh out of the ground. They were so sweet, delicate, and crunchy that they barely warranted any culinary attention whatsoever, but rarely will food miles be so few.

Makes 8

Preparation time: 30 minutes
Cooking time: 20 minutes

8 white asparagus spears

3 eggs

Scant ½ cup milk

Small bunch of chives, finely chopped

Salt

8 slices of Bayonne ham or prosciutto

Prepare a large bowl of ice water.

Trim the tough ends from the asparagus spears and peel the lower part about 2 inches up the stem. Bring a large saucepan of salted water to a boil. Add the asparagus to the boiling water and blanch for 4 to 5 minutes, until they are just tender (test with a sharp knife). Plunge into the ice water.

Heat a large nonstick frying pan over medium-high heat. In a bowl, whisk together the eggs, milk, chives, and a pinch of salt. When the pan is hot, remove from the heat, pour in a small ladleful of the egg mixture, and quickly swirl around the pan to make a large pancake. Return the pan to the heat and cook for a couple of minutes. Using a palette knife, gently peel back the pancake and turn it over. Cook for another couple of minutes, or until lightly golden. Repeat with the rest of the batter. Keep the pancakes on a plate and cover with foil while you make the rest.

Cut each pancake in half and wrap one half and a slice of Bayonne ham around each asparagus stem. This can be cooked a day in advance, kept in the refrigerator, and eaten cold.

Les petites astuces—tips You can replace the chives with any other aromatic herbs you might have, such as dill, parsley, or marjoram.

If you want to keep this vegetarian, add a handful of finely grated cheese to the egg mixture and omit the ham.

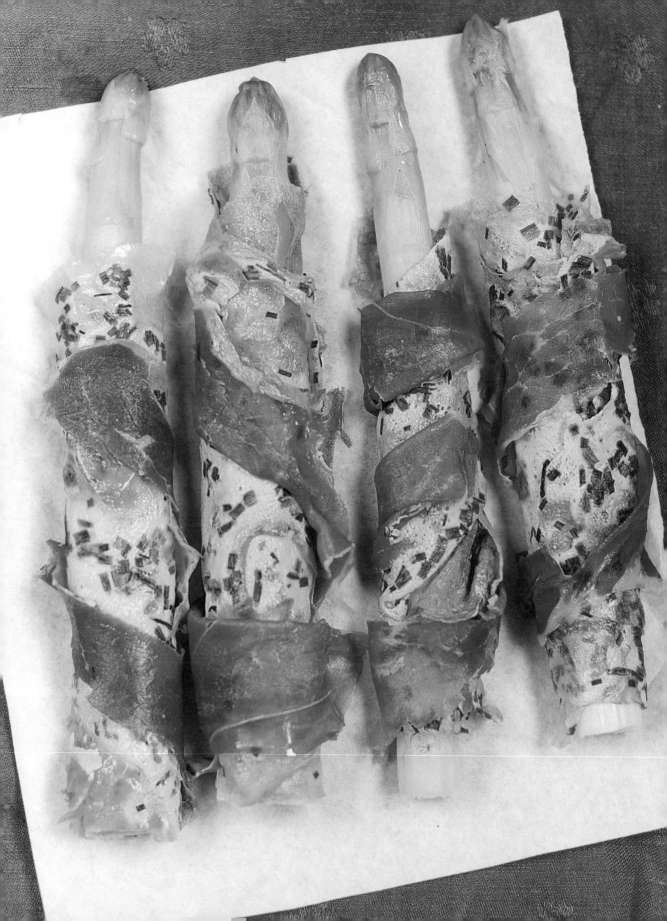

Baguette aux goujons et purée de petits pois

BAGUETTE WITH FISH FINGERS AND PEA PURÉE

Bordeaux and Britain share a love affair that started back in the twelfth century, when Duchess Eleanor of Aquitaine married Count Henry Platagenet, who then became King Henry II of England. The wine trade flourished during this period, and England remained a big importer of claret up until the Battle of Castillon in 1453, when France annexed Bourdeaux. I wanted to pay tribute to this Franco-Anglo connection, and what better way than with the marriage of the baguette with one of my guilty pleasures: fish fingers.

Serves 4 as a snack
Preparation time: 15 minutes
Cooking time: 15 to 20 minutes

For the pea purée

2 tbsp butter

1 shallot, finely sliced

1 clove of garlic, minced

1¾ cups/250 g frozen peas

3½ tbsp hot chicken or vegetable stock

Salt

1 tsp lemon juice

1 tsp lemon zest

Pinch of sugar

9 oz/250 g firm white fish (pollock, cod, or monkfish), skinned and boned

4 tbsp/30 g all-purpose flour

Salt and freshly ground black pepper

2 egg whites, lightly beaten

½ cup/50 g fresh white breadcrumbs

2 tbsp sunflower or vegetable oil

1 baguette

½ lemon

Generous 4 tbsp/60 ml crème fraîche

To make the pea purée: In a saucepan set over medium heat, melt the butter, then add the shallot and garlic and gently fry until soft and translucent. Throw in the peas and cook until the peas are soft. Add the hot stock and remove from the heat. Blend to a smooth paste in a food processor. Season with salt and add the lemon juice, lemon zest, and sugar.

Cut the fish into finger-size pieces and pat dry with a paper towel. Arrange three plates or shallow bowls in front of you. Pour the flour into one and season with a pinch of salt and pepper. Pour the egg whites into another, and spread out the breadcrumbs on the third. Dip the fish pieces in the flour and dust off any excess. Dip each piece in the egg whites and then roll in the breadcrumbs, making sure the fish is well coated.

Heat the oil in a large frying pan. Once shimmering, add the fish fingers (you may have to fry them in batches—don't overcrowd the pan) and cook for about 3 minutes in total, turning halfway through cooking, until they are a deep golden brown. Place the fish on a wire rack.

Cut the baguette in half lengthwise. Zest ½ tsp of zest from the lemon half and then cut the lemon into four pieces. Mix the lemon zest with the crème fraîche and spread it along one side of the baguette. Spread the pea purée along the other side and place the fish in the middle. Cut the sandwich into quarters and serve with the lemon wedges on the side.

Tourin à la tomate et perles du Japon

ROASTED TOMATO SOUP WITH TAPIOCA

If you feel a cold coming on, a classic *tourin à l'ail* is very much called for. Quite simply a garlic soup with tapioca or vermicelli noodles, some variations call for as many as twenty cloves of garlic, while others opt for onions. When tomatoes are in their prime season, this version makes their sweet acidity sing, capturing sunshine in a bowl. My version uses the juice of fresh tomatoes and the intense sweetness of slow-roasted ones. Throw in some "Japanese pearls" (the French term sounds so much better than *tapioca*) and you'll have a delicious dish that celebrates the season.

Serves 4

Preparation time: 30 minutes
Cooking time: 1 hour

1⅔ lb/750 g large ripe tomatoes

18 oz/500 g tomatoes, assorted sizes and colors

3 to 4 tbsp olive oil

1 clove of garlic, crushed

Sea salt

½ cup/100 g tapioca

1 green onion, finely chopped

Blend the large tomatoes in a food processor until smooth. Line a sieve with two layers of muslin or a clean tea towel and place the sieve over a large bowl. Pour half the tomato purée into the lined sieve. Gather the ends of the fabric and squeeze out all the juice. Scrape out and discard the pulp and repeat with the rest of the tomato purée. Set aside.

Preheat the oven to 250°F. Halve any cherry tomatoes and slice or quarter the larger ones. Place in a bowl and toss in 2 tbsp of the oil and the garlic, and sprinkle with sea salt. Arrange the tomato pieces on a baking sheet and bake for 1 hour.

Meanwhile, bring a pot of water to a boil and cook the tapioca until tender.

Divide the tomato juice, tapioca, and roasted tomatoes between serving bowls. Sprinkle the green onion over the top and drizzle with the remaining oil to serve.

Une petite astuce—tip Try not to blend the tomatoes for too long as this will result in lots of froth, which will make the juice cloudy. If you do get froth on the top of the juice, simply pass it back through a sieve.

Faire en avance—get ahead The tomato juice can be prepared 2 days in advance and kept refrigerated. Combine with the other components just before serving for a chilled soup.

Poule-au-pot avec riz d'ail croustillant

CHICKEN IN A POT WITH CRISPY GARLIC RICE

A chicken cooking in a pot is still the very essence of home cooking in the Bordeaux region, and how I first experienced it when I stayed at Château Lestange. The *poule-au-pot* arrived at the table surgically dissected and arranged on a tray. Mustard and a dish of artfully arranged carrots, potatoes, and leeks followed, and I doused everything in white sauce. My version is a little more streamlined—I've replaced the sauce with a punchy cornichon and mustard relish. Crispy garlic rice adds a fantastic texture.

Serves 4

Preparation time: 30 minutes
Cooking time: 2 hours

1 whole chicken (about 3½ lb/1.5 kg)

2 onions, quartered

4 carrots, peeled and halved lengthwise

10 black peppercorns

5 juniper berries

4 bay leaves

10½ oz/300 g lean sausage meat

2½ oz/75 g chicken livers, rinsed, patted dry, and very finely minced

3 cloves of garlic, finely minced

½ tsp freshly ground pepper

1 tsp orange zest

1¾ cups/300 g basmati rice

2 tbsp butter

Pinch of salt

For the relish

Heaping 2 tbsp capers, drained and finely chopped

12 cornichons, drained and finely chopped

Handful of chopped flat-leaf parsley

Heaping 2 tsp grainy mustard

In a large pot, combine the chicken, onions, carrots, peppercorns, juniper berries, and bay leaves. Pour in cold water to just cover the chicken, cover, and simmer for 2 hours.

Meanwhile, mix together the sausage, livers, one-third of the garlic, the pepper, and orange zest. Mold into a fat sausage shape on a large piece of foil. Roll up tightly and twist the ends to seal the foil. Prick the foil all over with a fork so the flavors can infuse the broth, then nestle it in the pot with the chicken (making sure it's submerged in the stock) for the last 30 minutes of the chicken's cooking time.

Put the rice in a small saucepan and ladle over 2½ cups of the hot stock from the chicken pot. Cover and boil over high heat for 7 minutes, then drain the rice through a sieve. In your largest nonstick frying pan (with a lid), melt the butter over medium-low heat and add the remaining garlic. Gently fry the garlic until it begins to sizzle, then stir in the rice and salt. Wrap the lid of the pan in a clean tea towel and place on top (the tea towel will absorb moisture so the rice stays crispy). Cook for 5 minutes on very low heat—you want the rice to crisp up on the bottom of the pan.

To make the relish: In a small bowl, mix together the capers, cornichons, parsley, and mustard.

Remove the chicken from the pot and cut into serving-size pieces. Unwrap the "stuffing" and slice into rounds. Serve each guest some crispy rice with the chicken, stuffing, and carrots. Ladle a little of the hot stock over the top and top with a little relish.

Monsieur Petit, free-range chicken farmer, Avensan

Poulet rôti au vin rouge

RED WINE ROAST CHICKEN

Even in Bordeaux, arguably the wine capital of the world, sometimes you can't quite finish a whole bottle. That's when this marinade comes in handy. A loitering leftover glass of red wine can make for the perfect marinade. If leftover wine is a rare occurrence in your household, donate a little glass from your bottle of red and enjoy a spectacular dish to accompany the remainder of the bottle.

Serves 4 to 6

Preparation time: 30 minutes

Marinating time: 30 minutes, or overnight

Cooking time: 45 minutes

⅔ cup red wine

6 tbsp/100 g tomato paste

3 sprigs thyme, leaves picked

3 sprigs marjoram, leaves picked, or ½ tsp dried

½ cup red wine vinegar

1 whole chicken, cut into 8 pieces (about 3½ lb/1.5 kg)

Salt and freshly ground black pepper

18 oz/500 g baby potatoes, washed

3 onions, quartered

6 carrots, peeled and quartered lengthwise

½ cup water

Mix together the wine, tomato paste, thyme, marjoram, and vinegar. Season the chicken with plenty of salt and pepper, then place in a sealed ziplock bag with the wine mixture. Shake the bag to make sure each piece is well coated. Refrigerate for at least 30 minutes, or overnight.

Place the potatoes in a saucepan of cold water, cover, and bring to a boil. Boil for 1 to 2 minutes, then drain in a colander.

Preheat the oven to 400°F. Arrange the onions, carrots, and cooked potatoes in a large baking dish or tray and pour in the water.

Arrange the chicken pieces, skin-side up, in a layer on top of the vegetables in the dish. Pour the marinade over the chicken. Cover with a sheet of parchment or foil and roast for 30 minutes. Remove the parchment and baste the chicken with the cooking liquid. Roast, uncovered, for another 15 minutes, or until the skin is crisp. Serve immediately.

Les petites astuces—tips Buying a whole chicken will always be more affordable. If you aren't up for dissecting it yourself, ask your butcher to cut it into pieces for you. If there's no knife-wielding butcher about, you can always cheat and go for chicken thighs.

If you're unsure whether the chicken is cooked through, pierce the flesh with a sharp knife; the juices from the chicken should run clear.

Faire en avance—get ahead The veg and chicken can be prepared up to 1 day in advance, then simply pop it all in the baking dish and cook.

Le Bouchon Bordelais, Bordeaux

Rouleaux aux canard croustillant et raisins aux Sauternes rôtis

CRISPY DUCK AND ROASTED SAUTERNES GRAPE WRAPS

Duck in France, particularly in the southwest where there are plenty of duck farmers, usually comes in the form of a confit (where the duck is cooked and preserved in its own fat) or pâté. Although delicious, making your own can be quite time consuming. I prefer to do away with the hassle of storing the duck in fat by simply roasting it with a few local ingredients, such as grapes and Sauternes, a rather unique sweet wine made in Graves, Bordeaux.

It just so happened that I was testing this recipe in my Paris kitchen on Chinese New Year. Living in Belleville, Paris's second Chinatown, I started thinking about the Chinese love of crispy duck. The roasted grapes in this dish are blended to make a sweet sauce (similar to the sweet plum sauce eaten with Peking duck). Wrap it all in a lettuce leaf with some crunchy cucumber and crisp fresh leeks, and you've got Asian-style French duck!

Serves 4

Preparation time: 20 minutes
Cooking time: 2 hours

2 duck legs

Salt and white pepper

9 oz/250 g seedless red grapes or prunes

Scant ½ cup Sauternes or other sweet white wine

½ cucumber or 1 small cucumber, washed, halved lengthwise, and seeded

1 small leek

2 tbsp olive oil

Juice of ½ lemon

Pinch of sugar

1 tsp hot chile sauce

1 romaine or iceberg lettuce, washed and leaves separated

Preheat the oven to 325°F. Season the duck legs liberally with salt and pepper, rubbing them into the skin. Place the duck legs in a baking dish with the grapes and Sauternes. Cover with foil and bake for 1½ hours. Increase the heat to 400°F, remove the foil, and cook for 30 minutes more (if the skin starts to brown too quickly, turn down the heat or remove from the oven).

While the duck is cooking, cut the cucumber into ½-inch cubes and slice the leek into thin rings. Soak the leek in a bowl of water for 5 minutes to remove any grit. Drain and dry with a paper towel before placing it in a bowl with the cucumber. Toss with the olive oil, lemon juice, and sugar and season with salt.

Once the duck is cooked, remove it from the tray and wrap in foil while you prepare a sauce. Put all the grapes and 2 to 3 tbsp of the cooking liquid in a blender and purée to a smooth paste. Add chile sauce and season with salt.

Peel the skin off the duck and chop it up. Shred or cut the meat from the bone. Serve the skin and meat with the cucumbers, sauce, and lettuce leaves and let everyone help themselves.

Crumble aux fruits de mer

OAT-CRUSTED SEAFOOD CRUMBLE

A savory crumble, I hear you ask? I questioned it too when I first spotted it on a restaurant menu in Paris. Who would have thought the French would steal a traditional British dessert recipe and make it their own? I wanted to combine some of Bordeaux's wonderful seafood with a classic British cooking technique. As tasty and comforting as a fish pie, but without the hassle of making a creamy sauce or mashed potato topping—that Parisian restaurant was on to a good thing.

Serves 4

Preparation time: 15 minutes
Cooking time: 30 minutes

5½ oz/150 g raw tiger prawns, peeled

5½ oz/150 g fillet of white fish (cod, monkfish, haddock all work well), skinned and cut into 1-inch pieces

4½ oz/125 g leeks, washed, trimmed and cut into ½-inch pieces

1¾ cups/125 g cauliflower, broken into ½-inch florets

1½ cups/350 g fromage blanc

1 tsp white pepper

1 tsp finely grated lemon zest

Pinch of salt

For the crumble topping

4 tbsp/50 g cold butter,
cut into small cubes

⅔ cup/75 g whole wheat flour

½ cup/40 g rolled oats

⅓ cup/40 g pine nuts,
roughly chopped

1½ oz/40 g mature Comté, Cheddar,
or other strongly flavored hard
cheese, finely grated

Preheat the oven to 350°F. In a bowl, mix together the prawns, white fish, leeks, cauliflower, fromage blanc, white pepper, lemon zest, and salt. Divide the mixture between individual ramekins or scoop into one large baking dish (about 8 by 10 inches).

To make the crumble topping: Use your fingertips to rub the butter into the flour until it has a sandy texture, then mix in the oats, pine nuts, and cheese.

Top the filling with an even layer of the crumble. Bake for 30 minutes, until the top is golden brown. Serve immediately.

Une petite astuce—tip Make sure that the cauliflower florets are the same size as the leek pieces; otherwise they won't cook through.

Faire en avance—get ahead The crumble can be assembled 1 day in advance and refrigerated until needed.

Brochettes de bœuf avec petits pains plats

BEEF KOFTAS WITH HERBY FLATBREADS

In the week before Shrove Tuesday, in a little town called Bazas, southeast of Bordeaux, you might stumble across a rather bizarre bovine occasion, when cows bearing flowers and ribbons on their heads are paraded down the main street. But these aren't just any old cows; they are the prized cult local breed Bazadais, known for the rich marbled fat running through the meat. The beef parade, which has been celebrated annually since 1283, culminates in a brilliant banquet with the Bazadais beef as the centerpiece. Inspired by this shared feast, my dish is a help-yourself affair; perfect for a get-together with friends.

Serves 4

Preparation time: 40 minutes
Cooking time: 30 minutes
Resting time: 1 hour
Equipment: 8 skewers (soaked in cold water if wooden)

1 recipe Flatbread Dough (page 275)

For the yogurt sauce
1 cup/250 g plain yogurt
1 tbsp lemon juice
Pinch of salt
Pinch of sugar

For the koftas
10½ oz/300 g lean beef, minced
2½ oz/75 g veal liver, finely minced or chopped
2 tbsp fresh breadcrumbs
Small handful of finely chopped flat-leaf parsley
1 shallot, finely chopped
1 clove of garlic, minced
1 tsp Espelette pepper or mild chile flakes
1 tsp lemon zest, finely grated
Generous pinch of salt
2 tbsp vegetable oil for frying

1 head of romaine lettuce, washed, dried, and finely chopped, for serving

Dust a work surface with a little flour. Divide the flatbread dough into eight pieces and roll out each one into a round about ¼ inch thick.

Place a nonstick frying pan over very high heat. Cook the flatbreads one at a time (unless you can comfortably fit two in your pan). Fry for 1 to 2 minutes, or until bubbles appear and the dough starts to color, then flip over and cook for another 1 to 2 minutes on the other side. Keep the flatbreads warm in a tea towel while you cook the others.

To make the yogurt sauce: Mix together the yogurt, lemon juice, salt, and sugar. Set aside until needed.

To make the koftas: In a large bowl, mix the beef, liver, breadcrumbs, parsley, shallot, garlic, Espelette pepper, lemon zest, and salt. Divide into eight pieces and squeeze onto the skewers. Heat the oil in a large frying pan over medium-high heat and fry the skewers for 3 to 4 minutes, turning occasionally until evenly cooked though.

To serve, cut open a flatbread, fill with a kofta and some crunchy lettuce, and drizzle with the yogurt sauce.

Croustade de pomme et boudin noir

CRUNCHY APPLE AND BLOOD SAUSAGE PIE

The *croustade* (also known as *tourtière*) is a popular Bordeaux treat, comprising layers of thin pastry sandwiching apples or prunes and doused with a sugary Armagnac syrup. My version uses some salty and creamy blood sausage, which marries beautifully with the tartness of apple.

Serves 4 to 6 as a starter
Preparation time: 45 minutes
Resting time: 1 hour
Baking time: 30 minutes
Equipment: a 9-inch round deep-sided cake pan

2 cups/250 g all-purpose flour

Pinch of salt

2 tbsp vegetable oil

½ cup warm water

5 tbsp/75 g butter, melted

4 tbsp/50 g sugar

1 tart apple, cored and sliced

7 oz/200 g blood sausage, skin removed

Mix the flour and salt together in a bowl, then pour in the oil and water. Using your hands, work the mixture until it forms a ball (add a few drops of water if it seems too dry). Knead until it is smooth. Wrap the dough in plastic wrap and let rest at room temperature for at least 1 hour.

Preheat the oven to 400°F. Place a clean fabric tablecloth on a large table and dust with flour. With your knuckles under the dough (palms down), gently start to stretch it out in a circular motion. When it's too big to hold, lay it down in the middle of the floured tablecloth. Use the same method to stretch it out, until the pastry is roughly 2 by 3 feet and paper-thin all over (you should be able to read a newspaper through it!). Trim the edges with scissors.

Brush 1 tbsp of the melted butter on top of the dough and halve. Brush one half with another 1 tbsp butter and sprinkle with 1 tbsp sugar. Fold in half, short edges together, and brush off any excess flour on the underside. Repeat with other half.

Place one piece of the pastry in the center of the cake pan, leaving the excess hanging over the edge. Brush with 1 tbsp butter and sprinkle with another 1 tbsp sugar. Arrange the apple slices over the pastry base and crumble the blood sausage on top. Place the second piece of pastry on top and tuck the excess pastry around and underneath the filling to encase it. Brush with 1 tbsp butter and dust with 1 tbsp sugar.

Fold the overhanging pastry from the base over the top, draping it into the center. Brush with the remaining butter and dust with the remaining sugar before baking for 30 minutes, or until the top and bottom of the pie are golden brown. Cool on a wire rack for at least 15 minutes before serving.

Gâteau aux carottes et noix de coco

CARROT AND COCONUT CAKE

Carrot cake can hardly be considered an authentic French cake, but with the rise of Anglo-American coffee shops around France, *le gâteau aux carottes* has rapidly become a regular fixture alongside scones and crumbles.

Serves 12

Preparation time: 30 minutes
Cooling time: 15 minutes
Baking time: 1 to 1½ hours
Equipment: a deep 7-inch straight-sided round cake pan

Scant ¾ cup/160 g soft butter

1 cup/200 g Demerara sugar

2 tsp ground cinnamon

1 tsp ground ginger

½ tsp ground cardamom

Finely grated zest of 1 orange

1 tsp salt

4 eggs

½ cup plain yogurt

14 oz/400 g carrots, peeled and roughly grated

3¼ cups/400 g whole wheat flour

4 tsp baking powder

For the icing

1 cup crème fraîche

2 tbsp confectioners' sugar

1¼ cups/100 g coconut flakes or shredded coconut

Preheat the oven to 350°F. Line the bottom of the cake pan with parchment and grease the sides. Using a stand or hand-held mixer, beat together the butter, Demerara sugar, cinnamon, ginger, cardamom, orange zest, and salt until fluffy. Beat in the eggs, one at a time, and then mix in the yogurt and grated carrots. In a separate bowl, mix together the flour and baking powder.

Fold the dry ingredients into the wet ingredients, then scrape the batter into the prepared pan. Smooth the top to create an even surface. Bake for 1 to 1½ hours, until a skewer, when inserted, comes out clean. Leave to cool in the pan before turning out onto a wire rack to cool completely.

While the cake cools, make the icing: Mix together the crème fraîche and confectioners' sugar until smooth.

When the cake is cool, use a spatula to spread the icing over the top and side of the cake, sprinkle with the coconut, and serve.

Les petites astuces—tips The whole wheat flour can be replaced with spelt flour for a lighter cake.

If you're in a rush (or prefer a lighter cake), do away with the icing and simply dust the cake with a little confectioners' sugar before serving.

Faire en avance—get ahead After cooling and before icing, the cake can be wrapped tightly in plastic wrap and frozen for several months. This cake is remarkably moist and will keep, un-iced, for up to 3 days.

Tarte tatin aux carottes

CARROT TARTE TATIN

Apples are the traditional choice of topping for a tarte Tatin, but carrots make a delicious savory alternative. Carrots are a staple in every French household, but they are not all the same. In the Landes region of southwest France, a particular type is grown that thrives in sand rather than soil. This makes for a flavorsome and juicy carrot, perfect for a simple dish such as this one where the carrot is the star.

Serves 4 to 6 as a starter
Preparation time: 15 minutes
Cooking time: 45 to 50 minutes
Equipment: a 7-inch round tart pan

8 to 10 medium carrots (or 5 large, halved lengthwise)

2 tbsp butter

3 sprigs thyme

Good pinch of salt

½ tbsp runny honey

1 tbsp red wine vinegar

9 oz/250 g puff pastry

Preheat the oven to 350°F. Peel the carrots if they have thick skins; otherwise, just wash them well and pat dry.

Melt the butter in a large frying pan over low heat. When the butter begins to sizzle, add the carrots and thyme. Cook for about 15 minutes, turning the carrots so they brown all over. Remove the carrots from the heat, sprinkle with the salt, and stir in the honey and vinegar so that the carrots are well coated. Arrange them in the bottom of the tart pan.

Roll out the puff pastry between two sheets of parchment until it is ¼ inch thick and cut out a disk that is a just a little bigger than the tart pan. Place the pastry on top of the carrots, and tuck in the edges. Cut a small cross in the middle (to let the steam from the carrots escape during cooking).

Bake for 30 to 35 minutes, or until the pastry is puffy and golden. Place a large serving plate on top of the pan and carefully flip the tarte Tatin onto the plate. Serve while still warm.

---

*Une petite astuce—**tip*** If you have a tarte Tatin pan or an ovenproof frying pan, you can cook the carrots in that and then tuck the pastry directly over the top.

Pruneaux au Cognac et épices

PRUNES IN COGNAC AND SPICES

The town of Agen, about an hour and a half drive southeast of Bordeaux, is famous for its prunes. Now, I realize that prunes don't have the best image—they are a little less glamorous than figs and not quite as fashionable as dates. But *pruneaux d'Agen* are a whole different matter; jet black and rich, they are considered such a delicacy that they even boast their own annual festival, the *Foire aux Pruneaux*.

Makes 1 large jar

Preparation time: 5 minutes
Cooking time: 30 minutes

18 oz/500 g pitted *pruneaux d'Agen*

⅔ cup Cognac or Armagnac

2 cups water

4 tbsp/50 g sugar

1 cinnamon stick

1 star anise

Pinch of salt

2 oranges, 1 zested and both peeled and sliced into rounds

Place the prunes, Cognac, water, sugar, cinnamon, star anise, salt, and orange zest in a saucepan and cover. Gently simmer over medium-low heat for 30 minutes, then remove from the heat and allow to cool.

Arrange the orange slices on a serving platter with some of the cooled prunes alongside. Serve immediately.

Une petite astuce—tip These prunes are very versatile and are great to have hanging around as a standby dessert. The syrupy juices can also double up as a sauce for ice cream.

Faire en avance—get ahead The prunes will keep well stored in an airtight container refrigerated for up to 1 week.

Gâteaux de la Dune du Pyla

SAND DUNE ICE-CREAM CAKES

Arcachon is postcard-pretty, sandwiched between the sweeping blue water of the Atlantic and a fragrant forest of pine trees. Inspired by the flavors and textures of this beautiful landscape, I sneaked some pine nuts into the base of my recipe for ice-cream cake.

Serves 6

Preparation time: 1 hour
Resting time: 2 hours
Cooking time: 20 minutes
Equipment: a 3-inch biscuit cutter

5 tbsp/60 g seedless raisins

3 tbsp Sauternes or rum

For the praline

6 tbsp/75 g superfine sugar

2 tbsp water

½ cup/50 g pine nuts

½ cup/100 g butter, at room temperature

5 tbsp/75 g light brown sugar

1 egg, beaten

¾ cup plus 1 tbsp/100 g self-rising flour, sifted

2¼ cups/540 ml good-quality vanilla ice cream, softened

10½ oz/300 g white chocolate

3 tbsp coconut oil

Soak the raisins in the Sauternes for 2 hours, stirring occasionally.

To make the praline: Line a baking sheet with parchment. Put the superfine sugar and water in a large saucepan and heat gently over low heat until the sugar dissolves, then increase the heat to high. When the mixture starts to bubble and darken, add the pine nuts and swirl the pan to coat them evenly. Pour onto the baking sheet and spread with an offset spatula (be quick, as it sets fast). Cool completely, then pulse in a food processor until it has the texture of coarse breadcrumbs.

Preheat the oven to 325°F. Cream the butter with the brown sugar. Add the egg and mix well. Then stir in the flour and most of the praline (set aside a little for decoration). Line an 8-by-10-inch baking sheet with parchment and, using a spatula, spread out the mixture until ⅓ inch thick. Bake for 12 to 15 minutes, or until golden. Using the biscuit cutter, press out six rounds and set these aside to cool completely.

Drain the raisins. Mix the raisins into the ice cream and, using a spoon and spatula, spread the mixture on to the biscuit bases, building it up to a peak. Smooth the edges with a spatula dipped in hot water. Freeze for 15 minutes, until firm.

Place the white chocolate and coconut oil in a heatproof bowl over a pan of simmering water (make sure the bottom of the bowl doesn't touch the hot water). Melt and stir together, then remove from the heat. Take the ice-cream cakes out of the freezer and ladle the topping over each. Quickly sprinkle with a little of the reserved praline and either eat straight away or return to the freezer, where they will keep for up to 2 months. Remove from the freezer 15 minutes before eating.

Crème brûlée á la semoule

SEMOLINA CRÈME BRÛLÉE

I love semolina pudding, but none of that hard, stodgy stuff. I prefer creamy, smooth semolina. There is something very comforting about savoring a little bowl of semolina, warm or cold, and at any time of the day for that matter. Here, I've decided to give it a little French makeover, studding it with juicy sweet prunes and giving it a golden, crisp crème brûlée–style topping.

Serves 4

Preparation time: 15 minutes
Cooking time: 10 minutes
Resting time: at least 30 minutes

2 cups almond milk or whole milk

2 tbsp/35 g semolina

4 prunes, cut into very small pieces

4 to 6 tbsp/20 to 30 g sugar

In a medium saucepan over medium-high heat, bring the almond milk to a boil. Add the semolina, whisking for 5 minutes, until the mixture has thickened. Remove the saucepan from the heat, stir in the prunes, then divide evenly between four ramekins. Chill for at least 30 minutes.

Just before serving, sprinkle an even layer of sugar over each ramekin. Do this by holding the spoon at least 12 inches above the ramekin (sprinkling from a height is the best way to create an even layer). Place the ramekins on a metal tray.

For best results, use a handheld blowtorch. Holding it 4 to 5 inches away from the sugar, move the flame slowly around the sugar, maintaining a steady, even motion. Stop torching just before the desired degree of caramel is reached, as the sugar will continue to cook for a few seconds after the flame has been removed.

If you don't have a blowtorch, take a large metal spoon and hold it in a gas flame until very hot (hold the handle with a tea towel or an oven mitt to protect your hand). Carefully place the spoon on top of the sugar and move it around so that the heat from the spoon caramelizes the sugar.

Serve immediately.

Canelé

Canelé are to Bordeaux what *kouign-amann* is to Brittany: an iconic sweet of the region, which sees every *pâtisserie* and *boulangerie* striving to create the ultimate version. The batter is not dissimilar to that of a crêpe, but the quality varies wildly between pastry shops, as I discovered in my quest to find the best. Traditionally baked in a hot oven in scalloped copper molds, *canelé* caramelize and crisp on the outside, while the inside remains pale and airy. My recipe will have you producing perfect examples every time, even without the copper molds.

Makes 14 to 16

Preparation time: 15 minutes

Resting time: 48 hours, or up to 5 days

Cooking time: 1¼ hours

Equipment: two 8-cup silicone canelé *molds*

2 cups whole milk

¼ cup/50 g unsalted butter, cubed

1 vanilla pod, split lengthwise and seeds scraped out

¾ cup plus 1 tbsp/100 g all-purpose flour, sifted

2½ cups/250 g confectioners' sugar, sifted

1 tsp salt

2 eggs, plus 2 egg yolks

¼ cup rum

Combine the milk and butter in a small saucepan with the vanilla pod and seeds. Bring to a boil over medium heat, then remove from the heat and let cool.

Combine the flour, confectioners' sugar, and salt in a large bowl. In a separate bowl, lightly beat the eggs and egg yolks together.

When the milk has cooled, remove the vanilla pod and set aside. Pour the warm milk and eggs into the bowl containing the dry ingredients. Gently stir together until smooth (there may be a few lumps at this stage).

Strain the batter through a sieve into a clean bowl, pressing through until you have a smooth batter. Add the rum and stir until combined, then add the reserved vanilla pod. Cover with plastic wrap and refrigerate for at least 2 days, or up to 5 days—this will allow the flavors to infuse and will relax the gluten, resulting in a tender, less chewy *canelé*. Give the batter a stir every so often.

When you are ready to cook the *canelé*, preheat the oven to 475°F. Heat the silicone molds in the oven for a couple of minutes, then, using a small ladle, fill each hole four-fifths full with the batter.

Cook for 15 minutes, then lower the heat to 375°F and cook for another hour. Remove the *canelé* from the molds and leave to cool on a wire rack. As they cool, the outside will develop a good crisp crust. Serve once cool to the touch. (Canelés turn spongy after 5 hours. To refresh, heat in a 450°F oven for 5 minutes. Cool until the crust hardens, then serve.)

Cocktail au Lillet, gingembre et citron

LILLET, GINGER, AND LEMON FIZZ

Lillet is an established favorite brand of aperitif founded in Bordeaux by the Lillet brothers. It's a blend of local Bordelais wine (Sauvignon Blanc, Semillon, and Muscadelle for the white variety, and Cabernet Sauvignon and Merlot for the red) with a hint of citrus liqueur, which makes it very refreshing. It can be drunk on its own, well chilled, or, how I like it, with some tonic water and a hit of ginger.

Makes 6 cups

Preparation time: 15 minutes

2 cups white Lillet or lemon vodka, well chilled

2 tbsp finely chopped crystallized ginger

1 lemon, sliced

6 basil leaves

Ice cubes

1 qt tonic water (optional)

Mix together the Lillet with the ginger, lemon, basil leaves, and ice cubes. Top up with the tonic water (or leave out if you prefer) and serve.

Une petite astuce—tip To make a frozen cocktail, simply pour the mixture (without the ice cubes and lemon slices) into a large container. Place in the freezer for 2 hours or until frozen around the edges. Use a fork to break up the ice crystals every 30 minutes. Repeat this several times before serving with lemon slices.

Basque

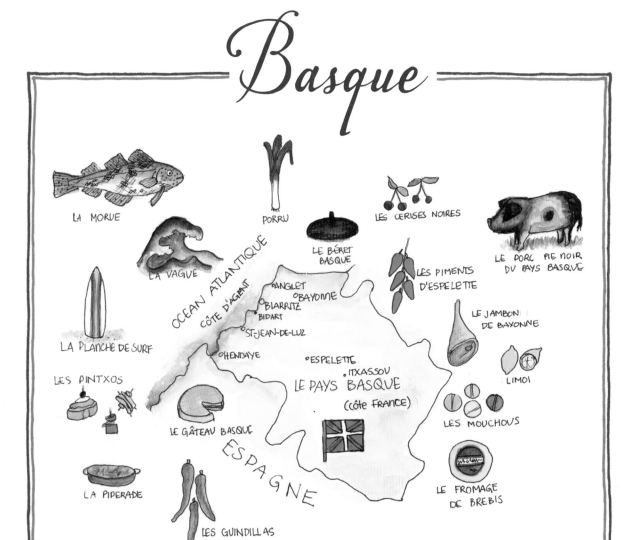

LA MORUE

PORRU

LES CERISES NOIRES

LE BÉRET BASQUE

LE PORC PIE NOIR DU PAYS BASQUE

LA VAGUE

OCEAN ATLANTIQUE

LES PIMENTS D'ESPELETTE

CÔTE D'AGENT

ANGLET
BAYONNE
BIARRITZ
BIDART
ST-JEAN-DE-LUZ

LE JAMBON DE BAYONNE

LA PLANCHE DE SURF

HENDAYE

ESPELETTE

ITXASSOU

LE PAYS BASQUE
(côte FRANCE)

LIMOI

LES PINTXOS

LES MOUCHOUS

LE GÂTEAU BASQUE

ESPAGNE

LA PIPERADE

LE FROMAGE DE BREBIS

LES GUINDILLAS

SURFERS' PARADISE, PINTXOS PARTIES, AND BASQUE KISSES

It was an early touchdown in Biarritz. Although it's only 1 hour and 20 minutes by air from Paris down to this nook on the Atlantic coast, at first glance the Pays Basque seems a world apart. It was mid-autumn, the rain was pelting down, and at 8 a.m. it was still dark and blustery. I headed off to roam the deserted streets in search of a hot drink and a sweet little something to keep me going on my explorations. From the ocean-facing windows at the historic pastel pâtisserie, Miremont, the day lightened to reveal an exceptional view of the craggy coastline, an odd surfer or two bravely bobbing in the water.

Biarritz feels quite literally exposed to the whims of weather. The waves crashed over the promenade, palm trees leaned at 45 degrees, and the gothic cathedral looked all the more imposing with swollen gray clouds clustering above it. But it is not just the landscape and exposure to the Atlantic that sets this extreme southwestern part of France apart; the Pays Basque is one of the most unusual and unique regions I visited.

Once part of the kingdom of Navarre, the Pays Basque was united with the Spanish part of the Basque region before it was split in the sixteenth century. This slight sense of segregation from the rest of France can still be felt, with various iconic symbols like the black Basque beret and flag, as well as road signs in both French and Basque dialect.

When it comes to the food culture, that's where things really start to get interesting (read: confusing). *Pintxos (*see page 104*)*, Espelette pepper, hanging legs of cured hams, and *planchas* are fundamental to the way the Basque French eat—items that rarely make a significant appearance in the rest of the country, as they are more closely associated with Spain.

Surprisingly for a nation that snubs spicy food, here in Biarritz—and even more so in the nearby village of Espelette—hot, plump red chiles reign supreme. Heading inland, the road to Espelette takes you up and down and into the mist-shrouded, lush green Basque hills. Farmhouses and sheep dot the countryside before Espelette appears before you with its bright white red-framed houses. The village's sole raison d'être seems to be tourism associated with the great *piment d'Espelette*. Strings of *piments* (Espelette peppers) hang everywhere: on hotels, houses, shop fronts, even the local chain supermarket. They make *gelée d'Espelette* (see page 127; lovely topped with a little *brebis* cheese), Espelette salt, purée, paste, lollipops— you name it. They even rub their hams with it during the curing process.

Among the Basque country's other idiosyncrasies are its eating habits—or, more specifically, *pintxos* hour. If ever a mealtime reflected a cultural attitude as a whole, this is it. Next to Biarritz's Les Halles (the famous food market) lies Bar Jean, a bustling establishment with young and old crammed in together, plates of *pintxos* piled high on the bar. The atmosphere is laid-back and welcoming; there is no room for Parisian pretentions or menu rigidity here. I was determined to re-create this *pintxos* spirit in a party at home (see pages 104 to 109).

Bayonne is a short drive from Biarritz, and is spectacularly set on the Nive River. The town is postcard-pretty, particularly in contrast to Biarritz's modern seaside resort architecture, with old higgledy-piggledy housing lining the river, all accessorized with brightly colored shutters.

Les Halles, the covered market, was filled with butchers, fishmongers, grocers, and bakers. However, it was the outside market that caught my eye. Producers from the region lined the river, showcasing fresh mushrooms, knobbly squash, gnarly tomatoes, and those ever-present *piments d'Espelette* in little woven baskets. Most of the market stands were tiny enterprises; one lady was selling only bags of dinky little apples for two euros a pop.

It was in this region that I discovered the French penchant for the bacon sandwich: a *ventrèche baguette*, with slices of bacon cooked on the *plancha*, piled into a baguette (see page 125).

The Pays Basque is famous for an eclectic variety of sweet stuffs, among them *Mouchous* ("little kisses"), Gâteau Basque (a controversial cake that we made at Le Cordon Bleu and not to everyone's taste), and chocolates. Macarons, like other things in the Pays Basque, are not as we know them. These are single-layered, ganache-free, rough and jagged like the Atlantic coast, but moist and chewy inside.

The Basque region is full of surprises, from its pervasive surfer vibe and social style of eating to its punchy seasonings and Spanish. With a little help from Espelette peppers, you can create some piquant condiments to spice up your pantry and bring some Basque style into your kitchen.

Pintxos salés à la Française

FRENCH SAVORY PINTXOS

Think *pintxos* and think Spanish tapas bar, a bustling help-yourself affair with high piles of nibbles impaled with sticks. Spanish and French cultures collide in the Basque region of France, where you are just as likely to find these delights as you are in San Sebastian, the home par excellence of the *pintxo*. Close to Les Halles, in Biarritz, I encountered an exemplary collection at Bar Jean, where groups of locals, young and old, were gathered at the bar, loading up their plates with a colorful array of these goodies. These are the ultimate party snacks: cooler than canapés, colorful, and quick to prepare, they are perfect for crowds and pretty much the easiest thing you can make for a cocktail party. At their simplest, they are an artistic assembly. All you need to do is raid your local deli counter and start skewering. Here is a selection of ingredients worth stocking up on for your savory *pintxo* party:

thin slices of Bayonne ham (or prosciutto di Parma, San Daniele, Serrano), chunks of chorizo, or other cured meats

cheeses: feta, Cheddar, mozzarella bocconcini, Roquefort, Gruyère

quail eggs (boil them for 2 to 2½ minutes)

cherry tomatoes

pickled mild chiles (often called *guindillas*)

olives (pitted, for practical purposes)

cornichons, caperberries, or gherkins

pickled beet and onions

jarred artichokes, mushrooms, roasted red peppers, or other grilled antipasti

anchovies (pickled or jarred/canned both have their merits)

a fresh baguette, cut into slices

Thread three or four different ingredients onto a cocktail pick or skewer. Allow for eight to ten *pintxos* per person. The following ideas are my favorite combinations. They all make eight, and take about 10 minutes to prepare.

BASQUE FLAG ON A STICK

8 pickled cocktail onions, drained • 8 pickled green peppers • 8 semi-dried tomatoes

Thread one of each of the ingredients onto a cocktail stick. Repeat until you have used up all the ingredients.

BAKED FIGS WITH WALNUTS AND CHEESE

8 ripe figs • 8 cubes of goat cheese • 8 walnut halves, chopped • 1 tbsp runny honey

Preheat the oven to 325°F. Line a baking sheet with foil. Cut a cross into the top of each fig, push a cube of goat cheese into each one, and sprinkle with walnuts. Bake for 10 minutes or until the cheese is bubbly. Drizzle a little runny honey on each fig.

HAM AND ZUCCHINI RIBBONS WITH MELON

1 zucchini • ¼ cantaloupe, seeded • 4 slices of Bayonne ham, prosciutto di Parma, or Serrano ham

Top and tail the zucchini, then run a peeler down the length of it to create eight thin ribbons. Set aside. Using a melon baller, if you have one, scoop out eight balls of cantaloupe flesh, or use a knife to cut eight equal-size cubes, about 1 by 1 inch. Cut the slices of ham in half lengthwise. Pop a cocktail stick into a cantaloupe ball, then thread a slice of ham in a ribbon on top and follow with a zucchini ribbon. Repeat with the remaining ingredients.

TUNA AND CRÈME FRAÎCHE BITES

4 tbsp crème fraîche • 5 tbsp/75 g finely chopped cornichons, plus 8 little sliced rounds for garnish • 1 tsp Dijon mustard • Good pinch of sea salt • 8 thin rounds of baguette • 1 can of good-quality tuna in spring water, drained

Mix together the crème fraîche, chopped cornichons, mustard, and salt. Roughly spread the mixture over the slices of baguette and top each one with a generous chunk of tuna. Add a round of cornichon and secure the whole lot with a cocktail pick through the top.

LITTLE GEMS WITH MUSTARD VINAIGRETTE AND GRUYÈRE

2 Little Gem lettuces • 2 tbsp grainy mustard • 3 tbsp extra-virgin olive oil • 3½ oz/100 g mature Gruyère or Comté cheese, cut into slices, or 8 thin slices of Bayonne ham

Remove the outer leaves from the lettuces. Trim the bottoms and cut both Gems into quarters lengthwise. Rinse and pat dry with a paper towel. Mix the mustard with the oil and brush onto the cut sides of the lettuce quarters. Place a slice of cheese or ham on top of each and secure with a cocktail pick.

SPICED OCTOPUS AND TOMATO CONCASSÉ

9 oz/250 g cooked octopus, roughly chopped • 2 tbsp extra-virgin olive oil • Pinch of salt • ½ tsp Espelette pepper • ½ tsp paprika • 2 large tomatoes • 8 rounds of fresh baguette, about ¾ inch thick • 2 chives, finely chopped

In a bowl, mix together the octopus, olive oil, salt, Espelette pepper, and paprika. Set aside. Bring a small pan of water (enough to cover the tomatoes) to a boil. With a small knife, score the bottom of each tomato with a cross. Plunge the tomatoes into the boiling water for 10 seconds or until the skin begins to blister. Remove and plunge into a bowl of very cold water. Peel off the skin and cut each tomato in half crosswise. Scoop out the seeds and chop the flesh into small cubes. Add the cubes to the bowl with the octopus and mix together. Divide the mixture evenly between the slices of baguette and garnish with the chopped chives.

Baked figs with walnuts and cheese
& Tuna and crème fraîche bites

Basque flag on a stick

Little Gems with mustard vinaigrette and Gruyère

Spiced octopus and tomato concassé

Ham and zucchini ribbons with melon

Cherry jam Lamingtons

Fresh fruit with chocolate dipping sauce
& Date and marzipan rolls

Frozen chocolate banana pops

Chocolate and cream buns &
Roasted pineapple, pistachio, and mint

Pintxos sucrés à la Française

FRENCH SWEET PINTXOS

As with the savory *pintxo* party, here is a selection of ingredients worth stocking up on for your sweet *pintxos*:

different kinds of fresh berries: strawberries, raspberries, blackberries	nuts	crème fraîche
	peanut butter	good-quality dark chocolate
chunks of banana and pineapple	chestnut spread	brioche buns
dried fruit: apricots, figs, dates	jam	madeira or sponge loaf cake

Thread your choice of ingredients onto a cocktail pick or skewer. The following ideas are my favorite combinations, but feel free to make up your own. They all make 8, apart from the Roasted Pinapple, Pistachio, and Mint, which makes 16. They each take about 10 minutes to prepare, but the Banana Pops need an hour in the freezer.

FROZEN CHOCOLATE BANANA POPS

4 bananas • 7 oz/200 g chocolate, broken into pieces • ¾ cup/75 g shelled hazelnuts, roasted and finely chopped

Line a large plastic container with parchment. Peel the bananas and cut in half to make eight short pieces. Carefully insert a wooden skewer (trimmed if necessary) into the cut end of each banana, up to the tip without pushing it all the way through. Arrange the bananas on the parchment and freeze for about an hour, until firm but not frozen hard.

Melt the chocolate in a deep bowl set over a pan of simmering water, stirring occasionally, until smooth (make sure the bowl doesn't touch the hot water). Remove the bowl of chocolate from the pan and dunk one banana at a time into the chocolate, coating evenly. Sprinkle the hazelnuts over the banana while the chocolate is still wet, then return the coated banana to the parchment-lined container while you cover the remaining bananas. Pop the bananas back into the freezer to firm up the chocolate, then serve.

CHERRY JAM LAMINGTONS

9 oz/250 g Madeira cake • 5 tbsp/100 g smooth cherry jam • ½ cup/45 g desiccated coconut, toasted

Cut the cake lengthwise into slices about ½ inch thick, then cut 1-inch squares from those slices to end up with 16 evenly sized pieces of cake. Using a teaspoon, coat each side of the cake squares with jam and sandwich two pieces together. Toss in the coconut to coat, then secure with a cocktail pick through the center. Repeat with the remaining 14 squares to make 7 more Lamingtons.

FRESH FRUIT WITH CHOCOLATE DIPPING SAUCE

8 strawberries, hulled • 8 blackberries • 1 kiwi, peeled and cut into 8 chunks • 8 Madeira cake squares, roughly 1 by 1 inch (optional) • ⅔ cup heavy cream • 3½ oz/100 g dark or milk chocolate, broken into pieces

Divide the strawberries, blackberries, kiwi, and cake squares (if using) onto cocktail picks or skewers. Heat the cream in a saucepan over medium heat, stirring to avoid it burning. When the cream starts to bubble, pour it over the chocolate. Leave for a few seconds and then stir the two together to form a luscious, thick sauce. Serve in a little pot next to the skewers for dipping.

DATE AND MARZIPAN ROLLS

8 firm, dry dates • 4 oz/120 g marzipan • 8 crystallized rose petals (optional)

Slice the dates in half lengthwise and remove the pits. Align the halves lengthwise, head to tail, on a piece of parchment, overlapping slightly at the ends. Fold the parchment over and, using a rolling pin, flatten the dates to about ⅛ inch thick and 3 inches long. Cut the marzipan into eight pieces and flatten each piece to the same shape as the date. Place a marzipan piece on top of a date and roll it up. Place a rose petal (if using) on top and secure with a cocktail pick. Repeat with the remaining dates and marzipan.

ROASTED PINEAPPLE, PISTACHIO, AND MINT

1 small pineapple • 4 tsp Demerara sugar • 3 tbsp finely chopped pistachios • 16 small mint leaves

Preheat the oven to 400˚F. Line a roasting pan with parchment. Peel the pineapple and cut it in half across the middle, then cut into quarters lengthwise. Trim out the tough internal core. Place the pineapple in the roasting pan and toss with the sugar. Bake for 8 to 10 minutes, or until lightly caramelized. Remove from the oven and cut each quarter into four chunks. Coat half of the pineapple pieces in pistachios. Skewer a piece of coated pineapple with a cocktail pick, add a mint leaf, then add a piece of uncoated pineapple and a second mint leaf.

CHOCOLATE AND CREAM BUNS

4 small finger brioche rolls • ½ cup crème fraîche • Sea salt for sprinkling • 16 squares of good-quality dark chocolate or ½ cup/110 g chocolate chips

Cut each brioche roll in half lengthwise. Spread 2 tbsp of the crème fraîche on the bottom half of each roll and sprinkle with a pinch of sea salt. Place 4 squares of chocolate or ½ tbsp of chocolate chips on each bun to cover the base. Then pop on the lid of the roll to make a sandwich. Place a grill pan over a medium heat. When the pan is warm, add the rolls. Use a spatula to press the rolls on to the pan to get nice grill marks. Turn over after about 45 seconds and cook on the other side. Cut each one in half and secure with a cocktail pick. Serve warm.

Sauce xipister

XIPISTER SAUCE

Every restaurant, bistro, or Basque household has a version of *xipister* sauce. There's no real secret; it's just about making use of the products in the region, combined to create a quintes-sential condiment. It's the Basque answer to Worcestershire sauce or soy sauce. Don't be shy using *xipister*; it adds a little lift to pretty much any savory dish and is great drizzled on meat, fish, or even pizza. It's also good used as a vinaigrette on salad. The quality of your sauce will depend on the quality of the vinegar and olive oil you use.

Makes: about 2 cups
Preparation time: 10 minutes
Resting time: at least 1 week
Equipment: a 1-pt glass bottle or jar with a lid

1¼ cups white wine vinegar or cider vinegar

⅔ cup extra-virgin olive oil

1 Espelette pepper or 1 medium hot chile,
washed and halved lengthwise

2 cloves of garlic, crushed using the back of a knife

1 bay leaf

1 sprig of fresh rosemary

2 sprigs of fresh thyme

Zest of 1 lemon

Place the vinegar, olive oil, Espelette pepper, garlic, bay leaf, rosemary, thyme, and lemon zest in the glass bottle, put the lid on, and shake well. Leave in a cool place for at least a week. Shake well again before using. The taste will get stronger the longer the ingredients are left to marinate. The sauce will keep in an airtight bottle or jar in a cool, dark place for a couple of months.

Piquillos farcis à la morue

PIQUILLO PEPPERS STUFFED WITH COD

This Basque dish is as a traditional as it gets. Delicious sweet little pickled peppers are stuffed with a lovely salt cod concoction. Salt cod, or *bakailao* in Basque, is hugely popular in Spain and parts of France; it's essentially a method of drying and salting cod to preserve it. If you track down salt cod for this recipe, rehydrate it in milk or water for 24 hours before rinsing and patting dry. Otherwise, use any cooked white fish.

Serves 4 as a main course
Preparation time: 10 minutes
Cooking time: 10 minutes

2 red onions, finely chopped

4 cloves of garlic, minced

½ tsp Espelette pepper (or more if you like it hotter)

1 tbsp olive oil, plus a little extra for drizzling

7 oz/200 g rehydrated salt cod or fresh cod, pollock, coley, or black bream, flaked

Juice of ½ lemon

2 tbsp finely chopped parsley

Salt (only if not using salt cod)

12 *piquillo* peppers (from a jar or can), at room temperature

Xipister Sauce (page 112; optional)

Fry the onions, garlic, and Espelette pepper in the olive oil until golden. Add the flaked fish and cook for another couple of minutes. Add the lemon juice and half the parsley. (Season with salt, if not using salt cod.) Stir together and cook until the lemon juice has evaporated. Taste for seasoning and add more Espelette pepper if you like it a little spicier.

Carefully open up each *piquillo* pepper and fill with the fish stuffing. Drizzle with a little more oil or *xipister* sauce and garnish with the rest of the parsley. Serve warm.

Plate hunting at a flea market in Bordeaux

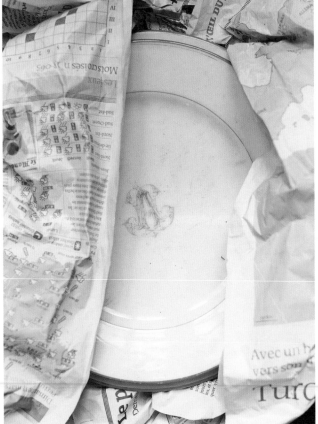

Tartines de tomates avec des rillettes de sardines

TOMATO SLICES WITH SARDINE PÂTÉ

Fresh sardines are abundant in the markets of Biarritz, so it's only natural to find them in many forms on menus in the local cafés, bistros, and restaurants. This recipe makes the most of the preserved kind, the best of which you'll find labeled as pilchards. Don't dismiss a canned sardine, as paying the price makes all the difference. There shouldn't be more than two ingredients on the label: sardines and olive oil. Traditionally, rillettes, a rough pâté, are served with crusty bread or toast, but tomatoes make a delicious gluten-free alternative.

Serves 4 as a starter or light snack
Preparation time: 15 minutes
Cooking time: 2 minutes

7 tbsp/100 g cream cheese, softened

1 shallot, finely chopped

1 tbsp finely chopped capers

2 tbsp finely chopped flat-leaf parsley, plus more for garnish

1 tsp lemon juice

Zest of ½ lemon

Pinch of Espelette pepper

Sea salt

Good-quality sardines or pilchards in olive oil (drained weight 3½ oz/100 g), large bones removed and oil reserved

1 tbsp olive oil

3 or 4 different colored, firm tomatoes, cut into ½-inch slices

Mix together the cream cheese, shallot, capers, parsley, lemon juice, lemon zest, and Espelette pepper and season with sea salt.

Use a fork to mash the sardines until it has a chunky texture and then stir into the cream cheese mixture.

Heat a large nonstick pan over high heat, and add the olive oil. When the pan is hot, add the tomato slices. Cook for 1 minute on each side, or until caramelized. Make sure not to overcook them, or they will become soft.

Remove the tomatoes from the heat and, when they are cool enough to handle, top each with a dollop of pâté. Sprinkle with the reserved parsley and drizzle with a little of the sardine oil. Serve immediately.

Une petite astuce—tip Choose firm, not overly ripe tomatoes that aren't watery; otherwise, when you come to cook them they will become mushy and disintegrate.

Faire en avance—get ahead The pâté will keep in the fridge in an airtight container for several days. You may need to use a fork to fluff the mixture, as it will start to set.

Porc et palourdes en cocotte

PORK AND CLAMS WITH CIDER AND LIMA BEANS

The Basque coast is a surfers' paradise. The rocky coastline is punctuated with stretches of windswept beach, much more rough and ready than its Mediterranean counterpart. I've always been an envious spectator of surfing, watching them gracefully (or not so gracefully, depending on their skill) catch and tame the waves whatever the weather. Surf 'n' turf is not what you would traditionally think of when it comes to Basque cuisine, but this is my homage to the Basque love of pork and to some gems from the ocean: clams. The clams are thrown in right at the end, adding a lip-smacking saltiness to the broth.

Serves 4 to 6 as a main course
Preparation time: 25 minutes
Cooking time: 2 to 2½ hours

2 tbsp butter

1 onion, finely chopped

3 cloves of garlic, crushed

2¼ lb/1 kg pork shoulder, tied

1 small bunch flat-leaf parsley

1½ cups dry cider

4 tbsp cider vinegar

1 qt hot vegetable stock

4 bay leaves

2 sprigs of thyme

4 small apples, peeled and cored

1 tbsp brown sugar

1 tsp sea salt

10 black peppercorns, crushed

2¼ lb/1 kg clams, cleaned

One 14-oz/400-g can of lima beans or navy beans, drained and rinsed

In a large pot with a lid, melt the butter over medium heat. Add the onion and garlic and fry until translucent. Add the pork shoulder and fry on all sides until golden.

Tie a string around the parsley stalks to make a tight bundle. Cut off the leaves (save them for later) and add the stems to the pot with the cider, vinegar, stock, bay leaves, thyme, apples, brown sugar, salt, and peppercorns. Bring to a gentle simmer and skim any scum that comes to the top using a slotted spoon. Simmer very gently for 2 to 2½ hours, until the meat is tender and falling apart.

Remove the meat from the pot, set aside in a tray, and cover with foil. Rest for 10 minutes. Pour the cooking liquid through a fine sieve into a bowl, discarding the strained bits. Rinse out the pot before pouring the cooking liquid back in. Bring to a boil and then add the clams and beans. Bring back to a boil, cover, and cook for another 3 minutes. Check that the clams are open and discard any that remain closed.

Shred the pork meat using your fingers or a fork. Serve with the clams, beans, and broth, sprinkling with the reserved parsley leaves.

Une petite astuce—tip Any leftover pork will be delicious in a roll with a dollop of hot spicy mustard: the perfect post-surf snack.

Batons d'aubergines pimentées avec couscous

SPICY EGGPLANT SPEARS WITH COUSCOUS

On a visit to the Saturday market in Bayonne, a picturesque town just twenty minutes' drive from Biarritz, I discovered lots of gnarly eggplants. But it wasn't just their gnarliness that captured my attention: some were a dark shade of purple, others pale cream, some were striped, and others speckled. Short, fat, and slightly misshapen, they were outcasts of the gastronomic world, those that never make it into our supermarkets. I threw them into my basket as soon as I spotted them, then promptly headed back to the kitchen and conjured up this dish.

**Serves 4 as a starter or
2 as a main course**
Preparation time: 30 minutes
Cooking time: 30 minutes

2 cloves of garlic

Pinch of salt

2 tbsp olive oil

1 tbsp tomato paste

1 tsp Espelette pepper

2 medium eggplants

For the couscous

Scant 1 cup/160 g couscous

Zest of 1 lemon

Pinch of salt

¾ cup boiling water

1 tsp extra-virgin olive oil

6 tbsp/100 g plain yogurt

1 tbsp lemon juice

Pinch of salt

Handful of chopped parsley
for garnish

Preheat the oven to 350°F. Line a baking sheet with parchment. Pound the garlic with the salt in a mortar and pestle until it forms a smooth paste. Blend in the olive oil, tomato paste, and Espelette pepper.

Cut the eggplants lengthwise into ¾-inch-thick slices. Cut each slice into ¾-inch-wide strips to make long spears. Throw away the spongy core. Brush the spears with the olive oil mixture. Place on the lined baking sheet and bake for 30 minutes, or until tender.

Meanwhile, make the couscous: Place the couscous, lemon zest, and salt in a large bowl and pour the boiling water over it. Place a large plate on top of the bowl and allow to steam for 5 minutes. Drizzle with the oil and fluff with a fork.

Mix together the yogurt, lemon juice, and salt in a small bowl. Taste for seasoning.

Pile the eggplant on a bed of couscous, drizzle with the yogurt sauce, and sprinkle with some chopped parsley to serve.

Une petite astuce—tip Pick eggplants that feel firm with a shiny skin.

Faire en avance—get ahead The marinade for the sauce can be made in advance and kept in an airtight container for a couple of days. The same goes for the yogurt sauce.

Sandwich au ventreche et ketchup Basque

BACON AND BASQUE KETCHUP SANDWICH

I spotted the locals in Biarritz gobbling down bacon sandwiches at a farming fair. It was the first time I had ever seen anybody in France eat bacon in such a quintessentially British way. I love sauce in my sandwich, especially when it packs a punch, so my version of ketchup is spicy, jammy, and slightly sweet, which, without a doubt, works wonderfully with fries, chops, fried fish . . . you name it. This recipe makes roughly 1¾ cups/450 g of sauce, enough for many bacon sandwiches.

Serves 4

Preparation time: 15 minutes
Cooking time: 40 minutes
Equipment: sterilized jars

For the Basque ketchup

1 tbsp olive oil

1 onion, finely sliced

5 cloves of garlic, crushed

3 bay leaves

1 Espelette pepper or a medium-hot chile, stemmed and roughly chopped

18 oz/500 g cherry tomatoes

1 peeled roasted red pepper from a jar, chopped

¾ cup red wine vinegar

¼ cup/50 g sugar

Salt

4 rolls, or a large baguette, quartered

8 thick slices of bacon

To make the Basque ketchup: Heat a small saucepan over medium heat, add the olive oil, and fry the onion, garlic, bay leaves, and Espelette pepper for about 10 minutes, until the onion begins to caramelize. Stir in the cherry tomatoes and roasted red pepper, cover, and simmer for 15 minutes.

Remove the bay leaves from the saucepan, carefully pour the mixture into a blender, and purée until smooth. (At this point it would make a great pasta sauce.)

Pour the sauce back into the pan and add the vinegar and sugar. Taste and add salt if required. Cook, stirring continuously, over medium-high heat for about 15 minutes, until the mixture reaches a ketchup-like consistency. Season with salt.

Spoon the ketchup into the sterilized jars and seal tightly. The ketchup will keep for up to 2 months, unopened, in a cool dark place or in the fridge.

Preheat the broiler. Place the rolls in the oven to warm. Arrange the bacon on a piece of foil on a baking sheet and place under the broiler. Broil for 5 to 6 minutes, until crisp, then flip and cook on the other side for another minute or so.

Slice the rolls in half and spread generously with the ketchup. Top with two slices of bacon per roll. Serve immediately.

Gelée de piment d'Espelette

ESPELETTE PEPPER JELLY

A cupboard staple in any Basque kitchen, use this jelly like mustard. It goes especially well with cheese.

Makes: about 1⅓ cups/400 g
Preparation time: 10 minutes
Cooking time: 25 minutes
Equipment: sterilized jars

1 oz/30 g Espelette peppers or medium-hot chiles

2 cups white or red wine

About 1½ cups/300 g sugar

2 tbsp/15 g pectin

Wash the Espelette peppers, remove and discard the stems, and finely chop the flesh. Place them in a pan with their seeds and the wine. Bring to a boil over medium-high heat and boil for 10 minutes. Remove the mixture from the heat and let cool completely.

Strain the cooled mixture through a fine sieve into a clean saucepan. Weigh the liquid and add the same amount of sugar.

Add the pectin to the saucepan and bring to a boil over medium-high heat while whisking continuously. Boil for 3 to 5 minutes, until the mixture coats the back of a spoon.

Pour the jelly into the sterilized jars and seal tightly. The jelly will keep for 6 months in a dark, cool cupboard. Once opened, it should be stored in the fridge and used within 4 days.

Terrine aux cerises noires

BLACK CHERRY TERRINE

Itxassou, a village just inland from the Basque coast, is where most of the region's famed cherries are from. There are numerous varieties: Xapata is a yellow-orange color and is the most acidic in taste, making it an excellent unadulterated, eating-straight-from-the-bag cherry; Peloa is a deep-red cherry, generally eaten raw; and finally, Beltza, the most famous deep, dark cherry of the region with its natural sweetness, is ideal for jam making. Traditional Basque cherry jam doesn't use pectin; instead the cherry pits are cracked and cooked with the fruit as they contain a natural gelling agent, which thickens the jam. This cherry terrine works as a dessert with whipped cream or vanilla ice cream; but as it's not overly sweet, it's equally delicious teamed with a creamy goat cheese or slivers of cured meats.

Serves 6 to 8

Preparation time: 10 minutes
Cooking time: 15 minutes
Chilling time: 4 hours, or overnight
Equipment: a 1-lb/450-g loaf pan

½ vanilla pod, halved lengthwise and seeds scraped

4 cups/425 g pitted jarred cherries, in their juices, or frozen cherries, defrosted

1 cup water

3 tbsp/40 g sugar

Pinch of salt

¼ oz/6 g leaf gelatin, soaked in water until soft

Line the loaf pan with plastic wrap.

Place the vanilla pod and seeds into a medium saucepan with the cherries and their juice, water, sugar, and salt. Over medium heat, whisk until the sugar dissolves. Bring to a boil, then take off the heat and cool for 10 minutes.

Remove the vanilla pod and discard. Squeeze the excess water from the gelatin sheets. Whisk the gelatin into the cherry mixture. Once the gelatin has completely dissolved, pour the mixture into the lined loaf pan. Refrigerate for at least 4 hours, or overnight.

When ready to serve, loosen the plastic wrap from the edges of the loaf pan, place a plate on top, and turn the whole thing upside down. Remove the plastic wrap and slice.

Serving suggestions

Sweet: Whipped cream, vanilla or dark chocolate ice cream, or shortbread and a dollop of crème fraîche

Savory: Creamy goat cheese and endive salad, or rich or fatty meats, such as *magret de canard* and *jambon*

Beret Basque au chocolat

CHOCOLATE BASQUE BERET

The black beret is the sartorial symbol of the Basque region; so much so that they even named a chocolate cake after it. A classic butterless genoise, doused in syrup and encased in a simple chocolate ganache, this is a serious chocolate bomb of a beret.

Serves 8

Preparation time: 30 minutes
Cooking time: 18 to 24 minutes
Equipment: a 7-inch round cake pan, at least 2 inches deep

½ cup plus 3 tbsp/120 g sugar

4 eggs, at room temperature

1 cup/120 g all-purpose flour, sifted

¼ cup/20 g cocoa powder, sifted

¼ cup/50 g sugar

3½ tbsp water

2 tbsp rum, kirsch, Cointreau, or amaretto (optional)

7 oz/200 g dark chocolate, finely chopped, plus ¾ oz/20 g, frozen, for garnish

Pinch of salt

¾ cup plus 1 tbsp heavy cream

2 tbsp/25 g butter

Candied orange for garnish

Preheat the oven to 325°F. Butter the cake pan. In a glass or metal bowl, combine the sugar and eggs. Place the bowl over a pan of simmering water (making sure the bowl doesn't touch the hot water). Whisk with an electric mixer until the mixture is very pale and almost tripled in size. This can take a while, so be patient. Remove from the heat.

Mix the flour and cocoa powder together. Sift a third of the cocoa-flour mixture into the egg mixture and fold in very gently. Repeat with half the remaining mixture, and repeat until it is all incorporated. Don't overmix or the resulting cake will be rubbery. Scrape the batter into the prepared pan and bake for 18 to 24 minutes, until a skewer inserted into the middle comes out clean. Turn the cake out onto a wire rack and cool completely.

Meanwhile, place the sugar and water in a medium saucepan over high heat. Bring to a boil. When the sugar has dissolved, remove from the heat and cool, then add the rum (if using).

Place the chopped chocolate and salt in a heatproof bowl. In a small pan over medium heat, warm the cream until bubbles form at the edges. Pour the cream over the chocolate and let rest for 2 minutes before stirring together with the butter until smooth (don't overstir or the ganache will become stiff).

Use a sharp knife to trim the sides of the cake to form a dome, then cut it in half horizontally. Place the bottom layer on a serving plate. Brush the cake liberally with the sugar syrup. Using an offset spatula, spread the cake with half of the ganache. Top with the other half of the cake and brush well with more sugar syrup. Spread ganache all over the cake, smoothing it. Decorate with grated or shaved frozen chocolate and a piece of candied orange before serving.

Crème au chocolat noir

DARK CHOCOLATE PUDDING

Chocolate has a long history in the Basque region, since the Jews, fleeing persecution in Portugal, first introduced it to Bayonne in 1609. By the nineteenth century, chocolate had become so popular that Bayonne boasted 33 chocolate ateliers with more than 130 chocolate masters. This chocolate pudding is rich and unctuous, but its richness is offset by the crème fraîche. It is delicious hot or cold.

Serves 6

Preparation time: 15 minutes
Cooking time: 15 minutes

1 tbsp/10 g cornstarch

¼ cup/50 g golden superfine sugar

Scant 1 cup whole milk

Scant ½ cup heavy cream

3 oz/85 g good quality dark chocolate, finely grated or chopped

2 tbsp butter, softened

Crème fraîche to serve

Pinch of Espelette pepper (optional)

Combine the cornstarch, sugar, milk, and cream in a small pot. Place over medium heat and whisk continuously for about 4 minutes, until thickened. When it releases a bubble or two, remove from the heat and whisk in the chocolate and butter. Divide between six ramekins or glasses. Serve immediately with crème fraîche and sprinkled with Espelette pepper, if desired.

Les petites astuces—tips Use a dark chocolate (around 70 percent cacao) for this recipe. Anything less won't give this pudding its rich chocolaty flavor.

Make sure to chop the chocolate finely. If the chunks are too big, they won't melt and your pudding will end up lumpy.

Don't leave the mixture to stand after cooking. Immediately divide it between the ramekins; otherwise lumps may form.

Bisous Chaumontais

CHAUMONTAIS KISSES

This recipe is the precious little offspring of a marriage between a *muxus*, a moist almond macaroon sandwich meaning "kiss" in the local dialect, and a *chaumontais*, a pastry made from cloudlike meringue with a golden hazelnut cream filling. While they were both a delight to eat on my visit to the Basque region, the *muxus* could have benefited from the traditional Parisian ganache filling, and the *chaumontais* were exceptionally enormous. So I thought I'd add a little Parisian finesse to these two classics and create dainty meringues with praline cream, easy to pop in your mouth. Just like kisses, you can't get enough of them.

Makes about 30 kisses

Preparation time: 30 minutes
Cooking time: 2 hours
Equipment: a piping bag with a ½-inch nozzle

2 egg whites

Several drops of lemon juice

½ cup/100 g sugar

1 recipe Praline (page 276)

7 tbsp/100 g butter, softened

Preheat the oven to 175°F. In a clean glass or metal bowl, whisk the egg whites and, when they begin to froth, add the lemon juice plus 2 to 3 tbsp of the sugar. Continue to whisk for another minute before adding a little more sugar. Repeat until all the sugar is used and the whites have formed stiff peaks. Scrape the meringue into the piping bag.

Line a large baking sheet with parchment. Pipe a dot of meringue under each corner to keep the paper in place, then pipe 1-inch dollops of meringue across the paper, leaving a gap between each one. Sprinkle a little praline on top of each meringue, then place in the middle of the oven and bake for 1½ hours. Leave in the oven with the door ajar for another 30 minutes before removing from the oven. Leave on the baking sheet until cooled completely.

Set aside 2 tbsp of the praline. Whip the butter until pale. Mix in the rest of the praline. Spread a small blob onto a meringue before sandwiching with another meringue. Once the meringues are sandwiched together, roll them in the reserved 2 tbsp praline so it sticks to the outer edge of the filling.

Provence

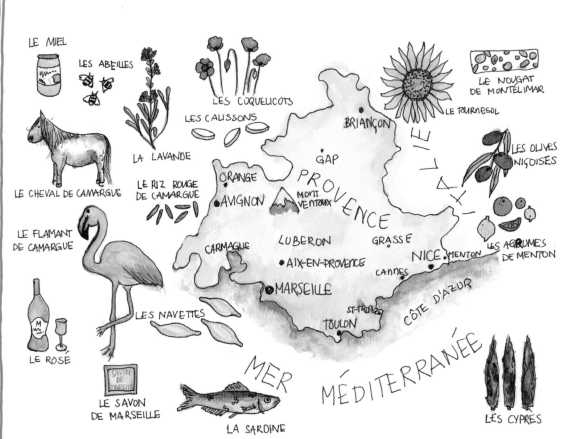

LE MIEL

LES ABEILLES

LES COQUELICOTS

LES CALISSONS

LA LAVANDE

LE NOUGAT DE MONTÉLIMAR

LE TOURNESOL

BRIANÇON

GAP

PROVENCE

MONT VENTOUX

ORANGE

AVIGNON

LE RIZ ROUGE DE CAMARGUE

LE CHEVAL DE CAMARGUE

LES OLIVES NIÇOISES

ITALIE

LE FLAMANT DE CAMARGUE

CARMAGUE

LUBERON

AIX-EN-PROVENCE

GRASSE

NICE MENTON

LES AGRUMES DE MENTON

CANNES

MARSEILLE

ST-TROPEZ

CÔTE D'AZUR

LE ROSÉ

LES NAVETTES

TOULON

LE SAVON DE MARSEILLE

MER

MÉDITERRANÉE

LES CYPRÈS

LA SARDINE

THE MENACING MISTRAL, FRAGRANT HERBS, AND ALFRESCO DINING

On the train from Paris to Nice at the beginning of November, the colors of the landscape changed from urban grays and cold blues to warm countryside browns and oranges before turning a dry, hot yellow with sparse patches of green. Once the train reached Marseille, it hugged the coastline, whizzing through St. Tropez and then Cannes, revealing glimpses of azure blue sea and palm trees, and finally arriving at Nice.

Nice was nice (with such a name it had to be), but I was more interested in visiting the olive growers in the hills behind the city. I hopped in my little rented car and drove off up the winding roads and down the narrow dirt tracks, often so tight that you had to honk your horn before going 'round a bend. I finally reached my destination: a wide expanse of luscious trees laden with ripe black olives. The Nice olive is not particularly big, but that doesn't mean it lacks punch. Considering its petite size it has a bold, peppery, fruity taste. The Nice olive boasts an AOC label, meaning it's protected against impostors and local quality is fiercely maintained; hence the olive oils and tapenades made using Nice olives are completely different from their Spanish or Italian counterparts, making them a little bit of a delicacy.

A beautiful drive along the coast farther east of Nice (I just needed a vintage car, headscarf, and sunglasses and I could have been starring in a movie from the 1950s) is the little town of Menton, on the border with Italy. Don't be surprised if you hear the locals speaking Italian as well as French at the market (Italians often do their grocery shopping in Menton). Menton has the perfect climate for citrus fruits, and lemons and oranges were just coming into season when I visited. The lemons are transformed into various products here: preserves, oils, mustards, savory spreads, liquor, perfume, soaps . . . this humble citrus fruit has rightly become a star of the tourist trade.

My second trip to the south didn't boast the stereotypical sunshine, but the famously ferocious mistral wind made itself known, howling at 80 mph around Marseille. I took shelter in the oldest homewares store in France, La Maison d'Empereur, which has been in business since 1827. It was a treasure trove of kitchen pots, pans, and gadgets: a true cook's paradise. A couple of minutes' walk away is the *vieux port*, the old harbor, where, when the weather is good, the fishermen (and women) rock up with their boats, tip out their catch, and sell it on the shore. There were plenty of little sardines to be spotted, although not one big enough to block the port, as the old story goes. In the eighteenth century, a large ship, *La Sartine*, was attacked near Marseille. Although badly damaged, the boat managed to sail into the harbor, where it promptly sank, blocking the harbor mouth so that no boats could go in or out. This had a devastating effect on people living there and the story spread throughout France. However, in its retelling, the ship changed from *Sartine* to *Sardine,* and postcards and posters depicting the Marseillais hauling a gigantic sardine from the port can still be spotted at antique markets and shops.

Marseille is unlike the rest of Provence; it has more similarities with Paris. It has a dynamic, cosmopolitan feel, thanks to its creative scene and the diverse range of ethnic groups that call the city home. The North African influence can certainly be felt, with numerous shops selling ingredients and housewares and a volume of restaurants specializing in spices, tagines, couscous, and sweet pastries. Heading inland provides quite the contrast. Here, the landscape still looks very much as it was depicted in the famous Provençal ochre, rose-pink, and lavender-colored pictures painted over a hundred years ago.

Just as the North African spices, such as *harissa* and *ras el hanout*, spike the air in certain neighborhoods in Marseille, the fragrant aroma of thyme and lavender greets you when you walk through the fields of Provence, brushing your legs against the wild flowering herbs. The range of different flowers provides an excellent food source for bees, and, as a result, Provence has a rich variety of honeys. Lavender honey is the most well known. Beehives are moved around during the warmer months to produce different types of honey.

When the menacing mistral wind has died down, sitting outside and enjoying a glass of chilled rosé is just the thing. To accompany the wine, food tends to be simple, with plenty of vegetables on the table (unlike the rest of France): a simply baked tian (see page 166), stuffed *petits farcis* (see page 144), or a colorful salad with fish (see page 151).

The flavors of Provence truly sum up the taste of summer for me. The fragrant aromas of the famous blend of Provençal herbs, colorful vegetables, a crisp refreshing glass of rosé . . . all best enjoyed outside. Even if the weather doesn't permit alfresco eating, you can still enjoy a little bit of Provence on your plate with this collection of recipes.

Ribs aux cassis avec couscous à la menthe et fèves

STICKY CASSIS PORK RIBS WITH MINT AND FAVA BEAN COUSCOUS

When I was a kid I would often make myself a black currant drink after school (usually with more cordial than Mum would like). Little did I know that I would be doing that when I was a grown-up, too. A dash of almost black, glistening crème de cassis with some Champagne and you have yourself a delicious Kir Royale (or just a Kir when paired with white wine). It's a very refreshing way to unwind after a long day. But it turns out it needn't be confined to the liquor cabinet. In a moment of inspiration, I reached for the crème de cassis thinking it would be perfect for making a sticky glaze for some pork ribs and, lo and behold, it was.

Serves 4 to 6

Preparation time: 30 minutes
Resting time: 1 hour, or overnight
Cooking time: 2½ hours

½ cup/160 g black currant jam

4 tbsp/85 g runny honey

½ cup crème de cassis

1 tsp freshly ground pepper

1 lemon, zested and roughly chopped

Salt

3 lb/1.5 kg pork ribs or beef short ribs

For the couscous

1 small bunch fresh mint, leaves and stalks separated

1¼ cups/200 g fresh or frozen fava beans

Salt

1¾ cups water

1 cup plus 1 tbsp/200 g couscous

2 tbsp olive oil

In a small bowl, whisk together the jam, honey, crème de cassis, pepper, lemon zest, and 2 tsp of salt. Place the ribs and chopped lemon with the marinade in a large freezer bag and seal it tightly. Give it a shake so the ribs are covered. Marinate, refrigerated, for at least 1 hour, but preferably overnight.

Preheat the oven to 300°F. Place the ribs, chopped lemon, and marinade on a rimmed baking sheet, cover with foil, and cook for 2 hours. Turn the heat to 400°F, remove the foil, and baste the ribs with the marinade. Roast for another 15 to 30 minutes, basting a couple of times. The sauce should become sticky and thick and the ribs should be dark and glossy from the sauce. Remove from the oven, transfer to a dish, and cover with foil. Pour the sauce into a saucepan and boil for 5 to 10 minutes, until reduced by half, then pour the sauce over the ribs.

Meanwhile, make the couscous: Roughly chop the mint stalks and place them in a pot with the beans, a pinch of salt, and the water. Bring to a boil, then pour over the couscous. Cover with plastic wrap or a clean tea towel and rest for 10 minutes. Remove the mint stalks, fluff with a fork, stir in the mint leaves and olive oil and taste for salt.

Serve the sticky ribs with the couscous.

Alfresco eating Provence-style

Rouleaux Niçois

NIÇOIS CANNELLONI

The French Mediterranean coast is the blessed land of the olive. One of the olive producers I visited, Champs Soleil, stood out in my memory not only for their fantastic olives but also for their organic vegetables: eggplants, peppers, tomatoes, zucchini. They combine the olives with the other vegetables to produce a range of tapenades that capture the sunshine-ripened flavors of Nice in a jar. These flavors are all packed into this recipe: black olive tapenade, grilled red peppers, ribbons of zucchini, and tomatoes. You might begrudge the use of pasta in a Franco-centric cookbook, but this is where France and Italy meet, and, despite their intrinsically stubborn nature, the French love a bit of pasta.

Serves 4 as a main course
Preparation time: 25 minutes
Cooking time: 20 minutes

18 oz/500 g cherry tomatoes, halved

1 tbsp olive oil

Pinch of salt

2 zucchini

8 large sheets of fresh pasta
(6 by 9 inches)

8 tsp black olive tapenade

7 oz/200 g roasted red peppers (from a jar), drained and roughly chopped

7 oz/200 g cooked artichokes, roughly chopped

⅔ cup crème fraîche

Freshly ground black pepper

1 small handful of flat-leaf parsley

Finely grated zest and juice of ½ lemon

Preheat the oven to 350°F. In a small saucepan, combine the cherry tomatoes, olive oil, and salt. Cover and cook over medium heat for 8 minutes, or until the tomatoes have burst and softened. Set aside.

Meanwhile, trim the zucchini and, using a peeler, make long ribbons. Stop when you get to the spongy seed core and discard.

With the short side of the pasta facing you, spread the tapenade thinly over them. Lay a few of the zucchini ribbons down the length of the sheets to just cover each sheet in a thin layer. Mix together the red peppers and artichokes and spoon 3 tbsp of the mixture down the center of each of the sheets, then roll the pasta up tightly from the long side, trapping the filling in the center. Place in a baking dish. Repeat with the other sheets of pasta.

Pour the tomato sauce over the rolled pasta. Season the crème fraîche with pepper, stir until smooth, and dollop over the top. Cook for about 30 minutes, until golden and bubbly.

Chop the parsley finely and mix with the lemon zest. Scatter over the cooked pasta and squeeze lemon juice over it all just before serving.

Les petits légumes farcis aux herbes de Provence

VEGETABLES STUFFED WITH RED RICE AND HERBES DE PROVENCE

When it comes to seasonings, nothing could be more quintessentially Provençal than *herbes de Provence*. Made up of savory, fennel, basil, thyme, and sometimes lavender, this fragrant blend works delightfully well sprinkled over vegetables and grilled meats, adding a little taste of the sunny south to the everyday. Camargue red rice is another of my favorite ingredients from Provence. It holds its shape and bite, adding an earthy nuttiness to whatever dish it graces. *Les petits farcis* is a popular Provençal dish of stuffed mixed Mediterranean vegetables. It originated as a way of using up leftovers.

Serves 4 to 6
Preparation time: 15 minutes
Cooking time: 45 minutes

¾ cup/150 g red rice, preferably Camargue

4 large plum tomatoes

4 round zucchini

4 small red or yellow bell peppers

4 tbsp extra-virgin olive oil

Salt and freshly ground pepper

1 red onion, finely chopped

2 to 4 large mushrooms, wiped

10 cherry tomatoes, roughly chopped

10 olives, pitted

1 tbsp chopped capers, drained

¼ cup/40 g raisins, soaked in warm water for 5 minutes and drained (optional)

2 tbsp dried *herbes de Provence* or a mixture of fresh herbs such as basil, thyme, and oregano

Bring 1½ cups water to a boil in a medium saucepan. Add the rice, lower the heat, and cook until al dente, about 30 minutes. Preheat the oven to 350°F. Line a baking sheet with parchment.

While the rice is cooking, cut the tops off the plum tomatoes and zucchini and use a spoon to hollow out the insides. Place the tops and the lower parts on the lined baking sheet. Cut the bell peppers in half and remove and discard their cores. Add the bell peppers to the baking sheet and drizzle with 2 tbsp of the olive oil and season with salt and pepper.

Heat the remaining 2 tbsp olive oil in a large sauté pan over medium heat. Add the onion and mushrooms and cook for 10 minutes. Add the rice, cherry tomatoes, olives, capers, and raisins (if using) and cook for 2 minutes more. Add the *herbes de Provence* and check the seasoning. Spoon the filling into the vegetables. Bake for 30 minutes or until the vegetables are slightly soft. Place the hats back on the zucchini and tomatoes to serve.

Une petite astuce—tip You can use leftover roast meat in place of the mushrooms, if you prefer.

Faire en avance—get ahead The stuffing can be made a couple of days in advance.

Farçous aux blettes et citron confit

CHARD AND PRESERVED LEMON BLINIS

Although *farçous* are originally from Aveyron, I first spotted one at the market in Montpellier, cooked by a little lady with a food stall, to be eaten on the go. It is a pancake packed with chard, and it's quite unlike your average French market fare, which usually consists of large vats of *choucroute garnie*, paellas, or rotisserie chickens. Only an hour after my first *farçou* experience, I was enjoying a gastro version in a smart local restaurant, Le Pastis, cooked by an ex-Paris-based chef, Daniel Lutrand, who champions the local produce. He served a delicate version as an amuse-bouche. Inspired by the preserved lemons that are popular in Provence, I've studded mine with little citrus hits; a lovely match with wholesome chard.

Makes 8 large or 16 small blinis
Preparation time: 5 minutes
Cooking time: 15 minutes

1½ cups/150 g all-purpose flour

1 tsp baking powder

Pinch of salt

1 shallot, finely chopped

1 clove of garlic, finely minced

½ tbsp finely chopped preserved lemon

3 chard leaves, finely chopped

¾ cup plus 1 tbsp milk

2 eggs, beaten

2 tbsp butter

Crème fraîche for serving (optional)

In a medium bowl, mix together the flour, baking powder, and salt. Add the shallot, garlic, preserved lemon, and chard. Mix together, and then stir in the milk and eggs.

Melt the butter in a large nonstick frying pan over medium heat. Use a spoon or small ladle to drop some of the batter into the pan and quickly flatten it down. Fry in batches (so as not to overcrowd the pan) for 3 to 4 minutes on one side or until golden brown before flipping and cooking on the other side for another 3 to 4 minutes. Serve warm, with a dollop of crème fraîche, if you like. These can also be enjoyed cold.

Une petite astuce—tip The chard can be replaced with 2 oz/ 50 g of baby spinach or kale, finely chopped.

Faire en avance—get ahead The blinis can be made a few hours ahead and reheated in the oven at 325°F for 15 minutes. You can also make the batter in advance and refrigerate it, covered, for 2 days.

Daube Provençale au rosé

PROVENÇAL VEAL ROSÉ STEW

The French love a good stew, so it didn't surprise me to spot a daube on menus—and even in jars at the supermarket—in Provence. There's not much that makes their version stand out from its regional cousins: cheap cuts of beef, a bottle of red wine, some vegetables and herbs. It does, however, have its own special pot, a *daubière*, which is made from clay and doesn't allow any steam to escape, keeping all the flavor trapped inside. I'm not sure whether a special pot will make a stew taste that much better, but the choice of ingredients, plus the magic of slow cooking, certainly will. Some of the flavors of Provence that I enjoyed most—blushing rosé, green olives, saffron, and fennel—replace the classic daube ingredients in my recipe. Serve with a big bowl of pasta (such as tagliatelle) tossed in a little olive oil or some baked potatoes.

Serves 4 to 6
Preparation time: 20 minutes
Cooking time: 2¾ hours

3 lb/1.5 kg veal shoulder, cut into large chunks

2 tbsp all-purpose flour

2 tbsp vegetable oil

2 onions, quartered

3 cloves of garlic, crushed

4 carrots, peeled

1 head of fennel, chopped (reserve the green fronds for a garnish)

2 cups rosé wine

3 cups water

2 pinches of saffron

10 black peppercorns

2 bay leaves

3 sprigs of fresh thyme

20 green olives

Sea salt

Dust the veal with the flour. Heat the oil in a large pot over medium-high heat and sear the meat until golden on all sides (don't overcrowd the pan; you may need to fry it in batches).

Transfer the veal to a plate. Add the onions and garlic to the pot and fry for a couple of minutes, until the garlic is soft. Add the veal, carrots, fennel, rosé, water, saffron, peppercorns, bay leaves, thyme, and olives to the pot. Cover and simmer very gently for 2½ hours, or until the meat is almost falling apart.

Remove all the vegetables and meat and set aside. Pour everything else through a fine sieve and then return the vegetables and meat to the pan with the stock. Season with salt. Sprinkle with the reserved fennel before serving.

Une petite astuce—tip The veal can be replaced with beef for a heartier dish or chicken for a more delicate flavor. Use a whole chicken that has been jointed and cook for about an hour (or until the meat starts to fall off the bone). The beef may need a little longer than the veal.

Faire en avance—get ahead Like all stews, this will taste even better if you make it the day before and allow time for the flavors to develop. Gently reheat for 45 minutes in a 325°F oven, stirring occasionally.

Joues de lotte de mer en croûte de noisette avec une salade

HAZELNUT-CRUSTED MONKFISH CHEEKS WITH A SUNSHINE SALAD

At the old port in Marseille you can find the local fishermen selling their catch—unless the waters have been rough the night before, in which case only the bravest fisherman will venture out. Among the sardines, red mullet, sea bass, and John Dory, you'll also find monk-fish. These fish are truly ugly, and look like they live on the bottom of the sea, but despite their scary appearance, I love them for their firm texture and almost boneless meat. Most people eat the tail, which is the meatiest part of the fish, but I'm a firm believer in "nose-to-tail" eating, and monkfish cheeks are lovely little bone-free nuggets of flesh. Like the tail, they have a substantial meaty texture, which pairs excellently with this crunchy nutty crust. Serve with a bright plate of sunshine salad made from carrot, grapefruit, and radish.

Serves 4

Preparation time: 20 minutes
Cooking time: 10 minutes

½ cup/50 g breadcrumbs

1⅓ cups/150 g finely chopped hazelnuts

8 monkfish cheeks

Salt and freshly ground pepper

1 grapefruit, zested, fruit cut into segments

4 tbsp/50 g melted butter

Olive oil for frying

10 radishes, finely sliced

½ watermelon radish, finely sliced

1 carrot, peeled into ribbons

2 to 3 tbsp extra-virgin olive oil

Combine the breadcrumbs and hazelnuts in a medium nonstick pan over medium heat. Toast until golden.

Season the monkfish with salt and pepper. Mix the grapefruit zest and melted butter into the toasted breadcrumb mixture.

Heat a drizzle of olive oil in a large frying pan over high heat. Place the monkfish cheeks in the pan and turn the heat to medium. Fry for 3 minutes, until golden, and then turn over and cook for another 3 minutes. Transfer the cooked cheeks to a plate and top with the breadcrumb mixture.

Toss the radishes, watermelon radish, grapefruit segments, and carrot with the extra-virgin olive oil. Season with salt and pepper. Serve immediately with the monkfish cheeks.

Les petites astuces—tips Don't dress your salad too far in advance. The salt will draw water from the radishes and make the salad watery and soggy.

If you can't find monkfish cheeks, you can substitute cod cheeks, allowing four per person. Alternatively, monkfish tail cut into ¾-inch-thick slices works too.

Nathalie   Rachel   Pierre   Lorena

Adrien   Antonin   Aurelien   Julie

Ratatouille en escabeche

RATATOUILLE APERITIF

In Paris, the first signs of sunshine at the end of the winter come via the markets. Even if it's still gray and cold, brightly colored produce from the south of France starts to appear. The pungent new-season garlic, the fat globe artichokes, and the deep purple eggplants are ideal served as an aperitif with some cheese and charcuterie, tossed with pasta, or on top of a pizza.

Makes 5 cups

Preparation time: 40 minutes
Cooking time: 15 to 20 minutes
Marinating time: 3 days
Equipment: a sterilized 2½-pt jar

1 red bell pepper

1 yellow bell pepper

1 zucchini, thinly sliced

1 eggplant, thinly sliced

Scant 1 cup extra-virgin olive oil

Juice and zest of 1 lemon

2 globe artichokes

1⅓ cups white wine vinegar

Salt

2 heads of garlic, cloves separated and peeled

2 tsp dried oregano

Pinch of sugar

6 fresh basil leaves

Preheat the broiler. Arrange both bell peppers on a parchment-lined baking sheet and place under the broiler. Turn every so often until they're blackened all over. Remove from the oven and seal tightly in a bag until cool. Remove the skin and tear the flesh into strips, discarding the seeds and core.

Heat a grill pan over high heat. Coat the zucchini and eggplant slices with some of the olive oil. Arrange on the pan (don't crowd the pan; cook them in batches) and sear until they have brown grill marks. Flip and sear the other side. Set aside.

Fill a large bowl with water and add the lemon juice. Trim the tips of the artichoke leaves, and trim the stalk. Peel away the dark outer layers of the stalk and the toughest outer leaves. Quarter, then scoop out and discard the hairy choke. Place the artichoke quarters in the lemon water until ready to use.

In a large saucepan over high heat, bring 1½ qt water to a boil with ¾ cup of the vinegar and a pinch of salt. Add the artichoke quarters and the garlic. Boil for 5 minutes, until the leaves are tender. Drain and place the artichokes and garlic on a clean tea towel.

In a small bowl, whisk together the oregano, the remaining olive oil and vinegar, the sugar, and a pinch of salt. Fill the sterilized jar halfway with layers of the vegetables, the lemon zest, and the basil. Top with the oil mixture and use a chopstick to release any trapped air. Repeat until everything is used up. (The vegetables should be submerged; if not, top off with a little more olive oil.) Marinate for at least 3 days. Store in a cool dark space for up to 2 months.

Ravioli Niçois grillés

PANFRIED NIÇOIS RAVIOLI

I lost count of the number of fresh pasta shops I spotted in Nice. The locals nip in on their way home from work to pick up a bag for dinner, and more often than not they choose *ravioli Niçois*. These ravioli are a pretty clever way of using up any leftovers from *daube Provençale*, as the slow-cooked meat makes a delicious filling alongside Nice's most popular vegetable, chard, and some local goat cheese. In my neighborhood in Paris, there are countless little Chinese dumpling bars. I love the contrast of textures in these dumplings: the crunchy base and the slightly chewy skin. These are delicious with Basque Ketchup (page 125) or Xipister Sauce (page 112).

Serves 4 to 6

Preparation time: 30 minutes
Resting time: 15 minutes to 2 hours
Cooking time: 10 minutes
Equipment: a 2-inch crimped biscuit cutter (or a glass)

2 cups/250 g all-purpose flour

¾ cup boiled water plus ⅔ cup water

2 cups/200 g leftover *daube Provençale au Rosé* (page 148) or Sunday roast

2 cups/50 g fresh chard or baby spinach

2 oz/50 g Tomme de Chèvre (rindless), mature hard goat cheese, or Parmesan cheese, finely grated

2 tbsp vegetable oil

Pour the flour into a large bowl and make a well in the center. Pour in the boiled water and stir together with your hands till you have a very crumbly, lumpy dough. (If the dough is very dry, add water by the tablespoon.) Transfer the dough to a flour-dusted work surface, and knead for about 5 minutes, until smooth.

Roll the dough in a little flour and place it in a plastic bag. Seal the bag and rest at room temperature for at least 15 minutes.

Meanwhile, finely chop the leftover *daube Provençale* and chard. Combine with the grated cheese.

Lightly dust the work surface and a large plate with flour. Divide the dough into quarters. Roll one quarter into a long rectangle, about 2 inches wide and ⅛ inch thick. Place 1 tsp of the filling 1 inch from the end and fold the end over to cover the filling. Press down firmly, making sure to press out any air pockets. Use the biscuit cutter to cut out a half-moon shape and trim the excess pastry. Place the ravioli on the plate. Repeat with the rest of the dough and filling, squeezing together the leftover bits of dough and rerolling once.

Heat the oil in a large nonstick pan until smoking hot, then add the ravioli in batches. Lower the heat to medium and cook for 2 minutes, until the base of each is golden. Add the ⅔ cup water, cover with the lid, and cook for 8 minutes, until the water evaporates. Serve immediately.

Millefeuilles au fromage de chèvre, fraises et concombre

GOAT CHEESE, STRAWBERRY, AND CUCUMBER MILLE-FEUILLES

Is this a starter, a dessert, or a cheese course? For me, it could easily masquerade as any of the three with its salty goat cheese, cooling and crisp cucumber, and sweet but ever so slightly acidic strawberries. This is a refreshing dish that I think transcends any rigid meal-time conventions.

Makes 6 mille-feuilles

Preparation time: 20 minutes
Cooking time: 10 minutes

6 tbsp/85 g butter

2 tbsp runny honey

4 sheets of filo pastry
(about 19 by 9 inches)

One 9-oz/250-g goat cheese log, crumbled

20 basil leaves

1 large cucumber

2 tbsp white balsamic vinegar

1½ cups/200 g ripe, firm strawberries, sliced

Preheat the oven to 325°F. Melt the butter and 1 tbsp of the honey together in a small saucepan. Place a sheet of filo pastry on a work surface with the long side facing you. Brush one-fourth of the butter-honey mixture over the pastry. Sprinkle 3½ oz/100 g of the cheese over it, then top with ten of the basil leaves (bear in mind that the sheet will be cut into ten rectangles, and there should be a basil leaf in each piece, so arrange the leaves in two rows of five). Place a second sheet of pastry on top and brush with more butter-honey. Cut the pastry in half lengthwise and then into ten rectangles and place on a baking sheet. Repeat with the remaining filo sheets (reserving the remaining 2 oz/50 g of cheese). Bake for 10 minutes or until the pastry is slightly golden.

Meanwhile, use a vegetable peeler to peel long cucumber ribbons (discarding the soggy core). Mix together the remaining 1 tbsp honey with the balsamic vinegar and toss to coat the cucumber ribbons, strawberry slices, and the remaining cheese.

When ready to serve, place a pastry rectangle on each plate and top with some of the salad. Top with another pastry layer, more of the salad, and a final layer of the pastry. Repeat to make the other five portions. (You will be left with two pastry rectangles, which you can eat like crackers.) Serve immediately.

Une petite astuce—tip Try replacing the strawberries with tomatoes.

Petits encornets au basilic avec pois chiches à la sanguine et tomate

BABY SQUID WITH BASIL, BLOOD ORANGE, TOMATO, AND CHICKPEAS

In the Luberon Valley is a village, Rousillon, where warm tones of yellows, oranges, and reds are everywhere. The colors and scenery have inspired artists for centuries, including Paul Cézanne, who was born in Aix-en-Provence and who produced numerous paintings depicting the local landscape. This region was particularly well known for its ochre pigments, mined from the natural stone in the region, and all the houses in the area are painted in similar earthy tones. The local cooperative, *ôkhra*, is keeping the tradition alive with educational workshops and a shop selling the traditional ochre pigments. Spot the colors of Provence in this dish.

Serves 4

Preparation time: 15 minutes
Soaking time: overnight
Cooking time: 1 hour

1¼ cups/250 g dried chickpeas, rinsed

4 tbsp olive oil, plus extra for drizzling

2 cloves of garlic, finely chopped

2 large tomatoes, roughly chopped

Salt and freshly ground pepper

9 oz/250 g baby squid, cleaned

2 blood oranges, peeled and sliced

12 basil leaves

Soak the chickpeas in cold water overnight. In the morning, drain. In a large saucepan, cover the chickpeas with water and bring to a boil over high heat. Boil for 45 minutes, until tender. Drain the chickpeas and rinse with cold water.

Heat 2 tbsp of the oil in a frying pan over medium-high heat. Add the garlic, tomatoes, and chickpeas. Toss and fry for 5 minutes, until the garlic is golden and the tomatoes are soft. Season with salt and pepper and pour onto a large serving plate.

Heat the remaining oil in the pan over medium-high heat and, when very hot, add the squid. Cook for a minute or two, until crisp but tender. Remove the squid from the heat, combine with the oranges and basil, and serve on top of the chickpeas. Garnish with a drizzle of oil.

Une petite astuce—tip If you can't get hold of baby squid, use large squid cut into rings.

Poisson et panisse

FISH AND CHICKPEA CHIPS

In Nice, they have a penchant for *panisse*-nibbling between meals. A chickpea-flour cake sliced into rounds, fingers, or cubes, fried, and then sprinkled with salt or dusted with confectioners' sugar for the kids, *panisse* can also pop up as an accompaniment to main courses or as a crunchy salad garnish. I love serving them as chips alongside fried fish and a spicy *harissa* mayonnaise, which gives a nod to Marseille's long history with North Africa.

Serves 4

Preparation time: 30 minutes
Resting time: 15 minutes
Cooking time: 30 minutes
Equipment: a 12-by-18-inch baking dish

2 cups water

1 lemon, finely zested and cut into wedges to serve

Salt

1 tbsp olive oil

2 cups/240 g chickpea flour

18 oz/500 g small fish such as sardines, anchovies, or herring

2 egg whites, lightly beaten

Vegetable oil for deep-frying

1 recipe Mayonnaise (page 276), mixed with 1 tsp *harissa* paste (optional)

Pour the water into a large pot and add half the lemon zest, a pinch of salt, and the olive oil. Bring to a simmer over medium heat, and then pour in 1 cup plus 2 tbsp/140 g of the chickpea flour. Stir with a wooden spoon while the mixture thickens, about 5 minutes.

Grease the baking dish and then pour in the chickpea mixture. Spread it out to ½ inch thick and refrigerate until needed.

Preheat the oven to 200°F and place a wire rack on a baking sheet or on the middle oven rack. Pat the fish dry. Place three plates in front of you: put the remaining chickpea flour on one plate, the egg whites on another, and leave the third empty. Dip the fish first in the flour, then in the egg whites, and again in the flour. Shake off any excess flour and place on the clean plate.

Pour vegetable oil into a pan to a depth of at least 1¼ inches, and place over high heat. The oil is hot enough if a small piece of bread dropped in sizzles as soon as it hits the oil. Gently place a few of the fish in the hot oil (do not crowd the pan). Fry for 2 minutes on one side; flip and fry for 2 minutes more, until golden brown. Transfer to the wire rack in the oven. Repeat until all the fish are fried.

Unmold the chickpea mixture carefully and slice it into ½-inch-thick chips. Be careful, as it will break easily. Bring the oil back to a high heat, adding more to the pan if needed. Fry the chips in batches until golden brown on all sides, keeping the cooked ones warm on the wire rack in the oven. Sprinkle the chips with salt and serve immediately with the fish, mayonnaise, and lemon wedges.

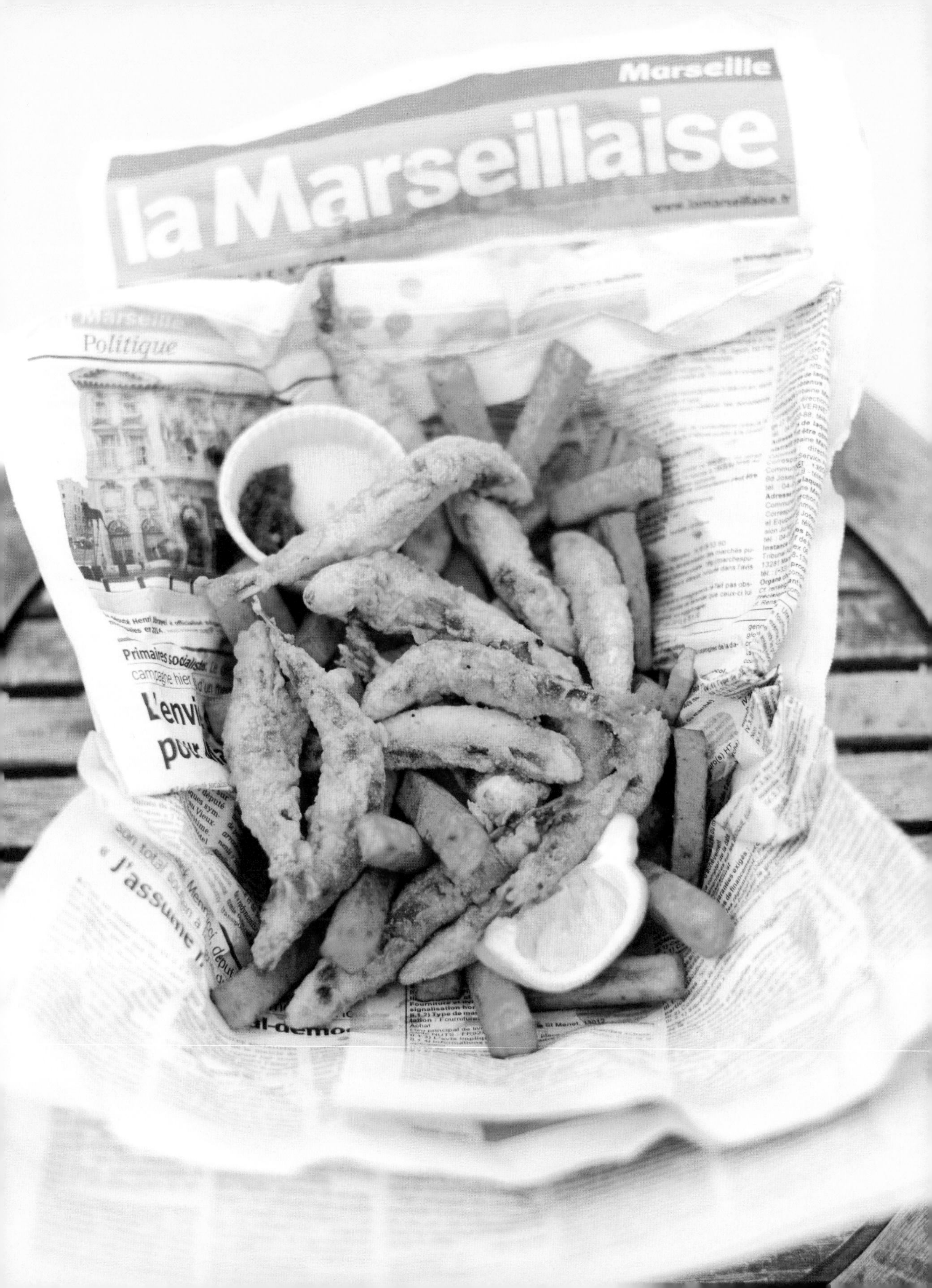
Marseille
la Marseillaise
Politique

Socca avec anchoïade

CHICKPEA PANCAKES WITH ANCHOVY SPREAD

Socca is Nice's answer to the Breton galette (see page 18) with the southern ingredient chick-pea flour replacing the northern buckwheat flour. I ate mine red-hot with a generous dusting of black pepper in Menton (a town just near the Italian border), which is *the* way to eat it (although you can sometimes spot the odd café serving it topped with salad and cheese like a crêpe). Cooked in a searing hot oven, the best *socca* are super-crunchy and charred from the heat. Unfortunately, the little oven in my Paris kitchen just doesn't get hot enough, so I get my frying pan as hot as I can to re-create a similar effect.

Makes 8 to 10 pancakes
Preparation time: 10 minutes
Cooking time: 20 minutes

For the anchovy spread

9 oz/250 g canned anchovies, drained

2 cloves of garlic

Zest and juice of ½ lemon

7 tbsp extra-virgin olive oil

Freshly ground black pepper

3⅓ cups water

Pinch of salt

2½ cups/320 g chickpea flour

4 tbsp olive oil

1 small red onion, finely sliced

Chopped flat-leaf parsley for garnish (optional)

To make the anchovy spread: Use a mortar and pestle to crush the anchovies, garlic, and lemon zest to a fine paste. Mix in the extra-virgin olive oil and lemon juice. (Alternatively, you can use a blender, which will make for a smoother paste). Season with pepper. The spread will keep for up to 4 days.

In a large bowl, whisk the water and salt into the chickpea flour to make a smooth paste. Refrigerate the batter for at least 1 hour, or up to overnight.

Rub a large nonstick frying pan with some of the oil, then place over high heat until very hot. Whisk the batter. Pour a ladleful of the batter into the pan and swirl it around (like you would when making a crêpe) and sprinkle with some sliced onion. Cook for a couple of minutes, until golden, before flipping and cooking on the other side. Transfer to a low oven while you cook the rest. Repeat until all the batter is used, greasing the pan with more oil before cooking each pancake.

Spread each *socca* with some of the anchovy paste and roll up or cut like a pizza. Serve immediately, sprinkled with parsley, if desired.

Une petite astuce—tip Use good-quality anchovies preserved in olive oil. If the ones you buy are very salty, rinse them carefully and dry them with paper towels.

Tian Provençal

PROVENÇAL VEGETABLE BAKE

If you have seen the animated film *Ratatouille* you will know that Rémy, the rat, shows the kitchen porter how to make a ratatouille. Real ratatouille connoisseurs, however, will have immediately recognized that it is actually not a ratatouille at all, but a typical *tian*. Both ratatouille and *tian* use the same vegetables; the main difference is in the cooking technique. A "real" ratatouille requires cooking the vegetables individually, before bringing all the elements together at the end; a *tian* is an artful arrangement of vegetable slices, which is baked like a gratin. It's a simplified, and more often than not better-looking, version of ratatouille.

Serves 6 to 8 as a side
Preparation time: 30 minutes
Cooking time: 40 to 45 minutes
Equipment: a 7½-inch round ovenproof dish

4 red onions, finely sliced

4 cloves of garlic, crushed

4 sprigs of fresh thyme

4 tbsp olive oil

1 eggplant

1 zucchini

5 firm tomatoes (plum tomatoes work well)

Pinch of salt

Preheat the oven to 350°F. In a large sauté pan over medium heat, fry the onions, garlic, and thyme in 2 tbsp of the oil for about 10 minutes, until soft and starting to turn golden.

Meanwhile, very finely slice the eggplant and zucchini cross-wise (1⁄16 inch thick). Use a mandoline or the slicer on the side of a box grater if you have one. Slice the tomatoes into 1⁄8-inch-thick slices.

Pour the onion-thyme mixture into the ovenproof dish and top with a few slices of the vegetables to make a flat surface. Arrange the rest of the sliced vegetables, alternating the colors, in a circular arrangement around the dish. Drizzle with the remaining 2 tbsp oil and sprinkle with the salt. Bake for 35 to 40 minutes or until the vegetables are soft and golden on top. Serve warm or at room temperature.

Faire en avance—get ahead This can be made 1 day in advance and eaten at room temperature or reheated in a 325°F oven at for 20 to 30 minutes.

Truffes aux chataignes et chocolat

CHOCOLATE CHESTNUT TRUFFLES

Provence celebrates the chestnut in all its glory, particularly during its peak season of late autumn, when village fêtes, featuring *dégustations* of roasted chestnuts and musical entertainment, come to town. Living in France has fueled my love of chestnuts, whether simply roasted, or in the form of *crème de marron*, the sweet purée featured in the Mont Blanc dessert. This little recipe is utterly addictive; these are perfect with a strong cup of coffee or for edible Christmas gifts. Try them once and you'll be finding any excuse to make them again.

Makes 18 to 20 truffles

Preparation time: 10 minutes
Resting time: 30 minutes
Cooking time: 10 minutes
Equipment: a kitchen thermometer

12 oz/340 g dark chocolate, finely chopped

7 oz/200 g cooked chestnuts

4 tbsp/50 g butter, softened

¼ cup/50 g sugar

2 tsp vanilla extract

Candied violets (optional)

Place 3 oz/85 g of the chocolate in a heatproof bowl over a pan of simmering water (make sure the bowl doesn't touch the hot water). Melt the chocolate and then remove the bowl from the heat and leave to cool a little.

In the meantime, blend the chestnuts, butter, sugar, and vanilla in a food processor.

Combine the melted chocolate with the chestnut mixture and mix well. Roll into walnut-size balls and refrigerate for 30 minutes. If the mixture becomes too soft to shape, chill for a few minutes to firm.

To coat the truffles, temper the chocolate (see Tip, below). Melt the remaining 9 oz/255 g chocolate over a pan of simmering water, as before. You want it to reach 115°F on the thermometer. Then, you need to cool the chocolate to 80°F. You can do this by placing the bowl over another bowl of icy water and stirring it until the temperature drops. The cooled chocolate must then be reheated to 88°F; at this temperature it is ready to use.

Dip the truffles in the chocolate and place them on a wire rack to set. Top each with a candied violet, if desired. Store, refrigerated, in an airtight container for up to 2 weeks. Bring to room temperature before serving.

Une petite astuce—tip Tempering chocolate gives it a lovely shiny finish and satisfying snap when you bite into it. You can temper chocolate in a microwave, but check it every 10 seconds or so with a thermometer so it doesn't overheat. When the chocolate has almost completely melted, remove it from the microwave and stir until smooth. It should have thickened slightly.

Tartelette Tropézienne

TROPÉZIENNE TARTLET

The *tarte Tropézienne's* reputation precedes it. The more I heard about this St. Tropez specialty, the more I started imagining something exotic with rum and tropical fruits. Actually, it's a basic brioche cake filled with pastry cream—simple but delicious. But if I had invented the *tarte Tropézienne*, this is how I would have made it.

Makes 8

Preparation time: 30 minutes

Resting time: 1 hour, or up to overnight

Cooking time: 1½ hours

Equipment: a pastry bag fitted with a ½-inch nozzle; 3-inch round biscuit cutter

½ large ripe pineapple, peeled and cut into thin slices

1 cup/100 g confectioners' sugar, sifted

3 egg yolks

3 tbsp/40 g superfine sugar

3 tbsp/20 g cornstarch

1 cup whole milk

½ vanilla pod

1 tbsp rum (optional)

8 thick slices of Brioche (page 218)

Heaping 1 to 2 tbsp very soft butter

Preheat the oven to 200°F. Line a baking sheet with parchment. Pat the pineapple slices dry with a paper towel and then dip them in the confectioners' sugar, making sure the entire surface of each slice is covered. Place the slices on the baking sheet, not touching, and bake for 1½ hours.

Remove the slices from the parchment as soon as they come out of the oven; otherwise they will stick to it. Cool on a wire rack.

Whisk the egg yolks with the superfine sugar until pale and thick. Whisk in the cornstarch until a trail is left behind on the surface when the whisk is lifted. Pour the milk into a small saucepan. Split the vanilla pod in half lengthwise and scrape out the seeds. Add the pod and seeds to the milk and place over medium heat; bring to a boil and then remove from the heat. Discard the vanilla pod and pour the hot milk in a slow stream over the egg mixture, whisking vigorously and continuously.

Return the mixture to a clean pan and continuously whisk over medium heat. Make sure to scrape the sides and the bottom of the pan, or it will burn. The mixture will start to thicken. Once it releases a bubble or two, take the pan off the heat and stir in the rum (if using). Pour the mixture into the pastry bag and refrigerate for at least 1 hour, up to overnight, before using.

Using the biscuit cutter, cut eight rounds from the brioche. Butter both sides, then place in a nonstick frying pan over medium heat. Fry gently for about 2 minutes per side or until golden. Flip the brioche onto a plate, pipe a thick layer of pastry cream on each slice, top with several slices of pineapple, and serve immediately.

Syllabub au rosé et aux fraises

ROSÉ AND STRAWBERRY SYLLABUB

If you have a soft spot for strawberries and cream, you'll love this posh version of the summertime classic. The south of France is blessed with sun-kissed strawberries, and they are an irresistible match for another fixture in the south: rosé wine. Fold the rosé syrup into a puffy cloud of Chantilly cream and you have a perfect alfresco dessert in a dash.

Serves 4 to 6
Preparation time: 15 minutes
Cooking time: 5 minutes

¾ cup rosé wine

6 tbsp/80 g sugar

½ tsp rosewater

Scant 1 cup whipping cream, very cold

Pinch of salt

2 cups/250 g strawberries, halved or quartered if large

Place a large metal bowl in the freezer to chill.

In a small saucepan over medium-high heat, bring the rosé and sugar to a boil. Whisk until the sugar has dissolved, then remove from the heat and let cool completely. Add the rosewater.

Pour the cream into the chilled metal bowl. Add the salt and whip to stiff peaks. Fold in the cool rosé syrup and half of the strawberries. Serve immediately with the rest of the strawberries on top.

Une petite astuce—tip For a nonalcoholic version, replace the rosé with apple juice.

Faire en avance—get ahead The rosé syrup can be made in advance and stored, refrigerated, for up to 2 months.

ARTICHAUT
"VIOLET de PROVENCE"

A visit to a
Provençal
wildflower and
herb garden.

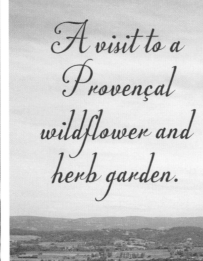

Le jardin
de nos
grands-mères

OUVERT UNIQUEMENT LE SAMEDI

Charlotte aux herbes et fleurs de Provence

MELON CHARLOTTE WITH CRYSTALLIZED FLOWERS

I'm partial to retro desserts, and you don't get much more retro than a ribbon-bound charlotte. When I was studying pastry, we piped and baked our own sponge fingers before trimming them to equal size to fit the cake pan. I've decided to take a shortcut and use store-bought lady-fingers instead. A ripe, perfumed cantaloupe is a great match for summer-scented basil.

Serves 8 to 10

Preparation time: 30 minutes
Resting time: overnight, plus 2 hours
Equipment: a paintbrush; 8-inch cake ring, or a springform cake pan with the base removed; 16-inch ribbon

1 generous handful of edible flowers such as pansies, violets, nasturtiums, and rose petals

1 generous handful of basil leaves

9 tbsp/120 g sugar

1 egg white, lightly whisked

¾ oz/18 g leaf gelatin

3 cups/500 g cubed ripe cantaloupe

30 ladyfingers

1⅔ cups whipping cream

Scant 1 cup/200 g fromage blanc

Line a baking sheet with parchment. Trim the flowers, removing the stems and the sepals. Set aside half of the flowers and basil leaves. With the other half, using the paintbrush and 3 tbsp of the sugar, brush each flower lightly with egg white, then sprinkle with sugar, holding the flower by the back of its head, or as delicately as possible if using rose petals. Shake gently to remove excess sugar and place each one on the sheet. Reserve 4 large basil leaves and coat the rest in the same way. Rest the flowers and basil in a cool, dark place overnight, until crisp to the touch.

Soak the gelatin in a large bowl of cold water. In a blender, purée half the cantaloupe with the 4 basil leaves until smooth. Pour the mixture into a medium saucepan over medium-high heat. Bring to a boil. Remove from the heat and let cool to room temperature. Squeeze the water from the gelatin and stir it into the cooled cantaloupe mixture until dissolved. Place in the fridge.

Place the cake ring on a serving plate. If the ladyfingers have rounded ends, cut one end so they are straight. Line the fingers around the inside of the straight edge on the plate ring, making sure they sit tightly together. If they start to fall into the ring, a second pair of hands may be required.

Whip the cream with the remaining 6 tbsp/80 g sugar until it forms stiff peaks. Beat the fromage blanc into the cold blended cantaloupe and then fold in the remaining cantaloupe. Pour the mixture into the cake ring. Refrigerate for at least 2 hours.

To serve, remove the ring and tie the ribbon around the cake. Decorate with the crystallized and fresh flowers and basil.

Bavarois au fromage blanc et rhubarb avec une tuile

BAVAROIS WITH AN ORANGE BLOSSOM TUILE

Navette is not only "boat" in French, but also the name of a very popular biscuit in the south of France. Most often perfumed with orange-flower water, these biscuits are somewhat hard and dry and are, as far as I'm concerned, an acquired taste. So I decided to make my own boat scene: a fromage blanc *bavarois* boat floating in a sea of cool pink rhubarb with a cookie sail.

Serves 6

Preparation time: 30 minutes
Resting time: at least 2 hours
Cooking time: 10 minutes
Equipment: six 3-oz ramekins or molds

For the bavarois

3 tbsp/40 g sugar

⅛ oz/4 g leaf gelatin, soaked for 10 minutes in cold water

2 egg whites

Scant 1 cup/200 g fromage blanc

½ tsp vanilla extract

18 oz/500 g rhubarb, cut into 2-inch pieces

1 cup/200 g sugar

For the tuile

4 tsp orange juice

⅓ cup/60 g sugar

1 tsp orange-flower water

Heaping 1 tbsp all-purpose flour

2 tbsp/30 g butter, melted

To make the *bavarois*: Put the sugar and 3 to 4 tbsp water in a saucepan and bring to a boil for 2 minutes. Make sure the sugar dissolves, then remove from the heat. Wait for the bubbles to stop rising, then squeeze the water from the gelatin and add the gelatin to the syrup.

Beat the egg whites until foamy and white, then very gradually pour the sugar syrup over them. Continue to whisk until soft peaks form. Beat the fromage blanc and vanilla together, then whisk it into the egg white mixture until just incorporated. Divide the mixture among the individual ramekins and refrigerate to set for at least 2 hours.

Pour ¾ cup water into a saucepan and add the rhubarb and sugar. Bring to a boil for 2 minutes before removing from the heat. Cool a little before refrigerating. Ten minutes before serving, place the syrup in the freezer.

To make the tuile: Preheat the oven to 350°F. Line a baking sheet with parchment or a silicone mat. Whisk together the orange juice, sugar, and orange-flower water. Sift in the flour while continuously whisking. Stir in the melted butter. Pour a ladleful of the batter into the middle of the lined baking sheet and spread the batter evenly, with an offset spatula, to 5 inches wide and ¹⁄₁₆ inch thick. Bake for 8 to 10 minutes. Remove from the oven and cool for 1 minute before cutting into triangles.

Unmold the ramekins onto serving dishes. Pour the ice-cold rhubarb syrup around them, and scatter some rhubarb on the plate. Place a tuile "sail" on top of each *bavarois* and serve.

Mousse au nougat

NOUGAT MOUSSE

Though a mainstay in the gift shops of Provence, nougat was a Middle Eastern invention. When it was imported to the port of Marseille in the seventeenth century, it quickly gained favor and Gallic production began. Olivier de Serres planted almond trees in nearby Montélimar, and soon the town became synonymous with the snow-white confection.

The key to good nougat is choosing your honey well. Provence is known for its lavender honey, which has a subtle flavor well suited to nougat. If you can't find lavender honey, another mild honey will work. I love the taste of nougat, but making it into a mousse is even easier than making the nougat itself, as no sugar thermometer is needed. In its mousse guise, you'll discover a light and airy alternative to its chewy cousin, but with all those nougaty flavors.

Serves 4 to 6

Preparation time: 15 minutes
Resting time: 1 hour
Cooking time: 5 minutes

2 tbsp/25 g shelled pistachios, roughly chopped

⅓ cup/50 g blanched almonds, roughly chopped

⅓ cup/100 g lavender honey or other mild honey

2 tbsp water

2 egg whites

¾ cup plus 2 tbsp whipping cream

¼ cup/50 g candied orange peel, finely chopped

In a small sauté pan over medium heat, toast the pistachios and almonds until golden. Place the honey and water in a saucepan over high heat and cook for about 5 minutes; the mixture will foam like crazy then calm down.

In the meantime, whisk the egg whites until frothy. Once the honey is bubbling gently, slowly pour it over the egg whites while whisking. Continue to whisk for about 5 minutes, until the egg whites form soft peaks. Set aside to cool for a few minutes.

Whip the cream to soft peaks. Set aside 2 to 3 tbsp of the pistachios, almonds, and candied orange peel to sprinkle on top of the finished mousse, then fold the rest into the egg whites, along with the whipped cream.

Divide the mixture between glasses or bowls and refrigerate for at least an hour, until well-chilled. Sprinkle the reserved pistachios, almonds, and candied orange peel on top before serving.

Une petite astuce—tip This dessert can be frozen into a *semifreddo*. Pour the mixture into a loaf pan lined with plastic wrap and freeze. Serve in slices.

Lyon

LE SAINT-MARCELLIN

LE PÂTÉ EN CROÛTE

LA NEIGE

LE BEAUFORT

LES SAUCISSONS DE LYON

SUISSE

LA FONDUE

LA PRALINE

LYON

ANNECY

SAINT-ÉTIENNE

CHAMONIX MONT BLANC

LES ALPES

ITALIE

LA NOIX DE GRENOBLE

VALENCE

GRENOBLE

RHÔNE

LE REBLOCHON

LE CHALET

LES COUSSINS DE LYON

LES QUENELLES

LA MONTAGNE

LE BROCHET

LA TOQUE

LE BOUCHON

THE ALMIGHTY FRENCH LION, SWEETMEATS, AND SNOWY PEAKS

Lyon is the capital of French gastronomy; the home of the godfather of modern French cuisine, Paul Bocuse, it has easy access to Burgundy and Côtes du Rhône appellations. It all sounds rather grand, but actually Lyon's reputation for good food comes from humble roots.

After the French Revolution of the nineteenth century, a number of women, many of them previously cooks for bourgeois families in Lyon, started serving meals to the *canuts* (the workers from the silk factories). *Les mères Lyonnaises*, as they came to be called, began opening eateries serving simple home-cooked fare that was impeccably prepared. It wasn't just the silk workers who came to eat their food; its quality and affordability attracted people from all different backgrounds. Some of the eateries gained reputations as great as any Parisian restaurants at the time: Eugènie Brazier was awarded Michelin stars in 1933—the first woman to receive such an honor and no small feat for any chef.

With all this in the back of my mind, Lyon had a lot to live up to. My first port of call was, of course, lunch at a bouchon, the traditional Lyonnais eatery. My first bouchon experience was no light matter, not only because I had high hopes, but also because I experienced, firsthand, the Lyonnais love of nose-to-tail eating and supersized portions. The meal kicked off with a lovely green salad with delicate lamb sweetbreads and an excellent dressing. It was followed by a classic Lyonnais plate of chicken liver pudding with tomato coulis and dumplings. Now, one would think that this would be enough, but accompaniments came fast and furious from the kitchen: a side of potato gratin, seasonal vegetables, macaroni, cheese, and a loaded bread basket. I barely managed to make a dent. Even though I was almost bursting at the seams, I couldn't resist going for one of my favorite French desserts, *île flottante*, a poached meringue in a pool of light custard. This one boasted a pink praline center, adding a delicious crunch to the dish from the caramelized almonds. I rolled out of the bouchon.

My next stop was Les Halles de Lyon Paul Bocuse, a food hall filled with specialties from the Lyon region. Sausages were strung up from the ceiling at the butcher's counter, large pink-stained brioches were temptingly piled up, oozy Saint-Marcellin cheese enticed at La Mère Richard cheese stand (the cheesemonger will ask when you want to eat the cheese and will select accordingly), and cylindrical quenelles, the artisanal Lyonnais dumplings, were neatly lined up everywhere. It was the ideal homage to Paul Bocuse, who invented the concept of nouvelle cuisine, a food movement that aims to showcase quality ingredients and offer a lighter and less opulent approach to dining.

Eating in Lyon certainly felt like a sporting event, and my stomach was stretched into new dimensions. Luckily the French Alps are only an hour away, providing the perfect place to work off those extra pounds and build up a new appetite from skiing and hiking. It's not about Michelin-starred restaurants on the slopes, of course, but wooden chalets, roaring fires, scoops of hearty *tartiflette* (cheesy bacon and potato casserole), and warming onion soup.

On my first night in the sleepy little mountain village of Peisey-Nancroix, Madame Chenal, the owner of the bed-and-breakfast I was staying at, served cheese fondue, the mountain classic, for dinner. Madame Chenal was quite the cook, making everything from scratch, from yogurts using milk from the local farm to homemade charcuterie, jams, cakes, and breads. Before transport became so accessible, this style of home production was fairly common in the more remote mountain villages; people had to be a lot more self-sufficient in their approach to eating, and Madame Chenal still embraces this ethos.

During my stay, I discovered other lesser known but equally enticing dishes and ingredients: little diamond-shaped buckwheat pasta called *crozet* (see page 204), mainly served as a gooey, cheesy gratin; a creamy smooth chestnut pumpkin soup; and an utterly luscious walnut and caramel tart (see page 223). And, as I happened to be staying over the Easter weekend, I also discovered the cutest chocolate rabbits hiding in my room!

Simplicity is key to the cuisine of this area, and, most of the time, a good mature mountain cheese like Beaufort or Reblochon was enough to keep me happy. But despite all the skiing I did during the day, I certainly didn't feel like I was going hungry at night.

Both Lyon and the bordering French Alps have wholesome home-cooked dishes at their heart, which, for me, is more inspiring than any fine-dining culture. Since I am an offal lover, Lyonnais attitudes to making use of every part of the animal suited me to a T and inspired a couple of dishes in this chapter.

Quenelles à la semoule

SAVORY SEMOLINA DUMPLINGS

Lyon is the capital of quenelles, or, as we have less graciously named them, "dumplings." The most famous of them all is the *quenelle de brochet*, which is made of pike. Testament to the city's obsession is the Bar à Quenelles, where you can grab a quick quenelle-on-the-go. They have many types, cooked in a variety of ways: panfried, steamed, or in a soup. I find that the simplest way is like the Italians cook their gnocchi: in boiling, salted water. There's really not much effort required when making quenelles, and most of the ingredients are pantry staples, making them the perfect dish to whip up in less than 30 minutes.

Makes about 48 mini quenelles
Preparation time: 10 minutes
Cooking time: 5 minutes

1 cup milk

3 tbsp/40 g butter

Salt and freshly ground pepper

Generous pinch of freshly grated nutmeg

1⅓ cups/140 g semolina flour

2 egg yolks

Optional flavorings

¾ cup/140 g drained cooked spinach, blended to a smooth paste

2 oz/50 g strongly flavored cheese, grated

2 to 3 tsp sun-dried tomato paste

Extra-virgin olive oil for drizzling

Grated strongly flavored cheese for serving (optional)

Put the milk, butter, a pinch of salt and pepper, and the nutmeg in a pan and bring to a boil. Remove from the heat and, using a wooden spoon, beat in the semolina with the egg yolks. At this point, beat in one of the flavorings (if using). Make sure to beat hard and fast; otherwise the semolina will become lumpy. Stir until it comes together into a smooth dough.

Dust a plate or baking sheet with semolina. Use two teaspoons to form the dough into a quenelle shape and rest it on the plate while you finish forming the others.

Bring a large saucepan of water with a generous pinch of salt to a boil. Add all the dumplings. As soon as they rise to the top, use a slotted spoon to remove them from the water. Drain well and serve drizzled with a little oil and a sprinkling of cheese, if you like.

Une petite astuce—tip Dip the teaspoons in warm water between each scoop; this will keep the mixture from sticking.

Faire en avance—get ahead Dust some plastic wrap with semolina flour and roll the dough into a long snaky length about ¾ inch in diameter. Cut into ¾-inch pieces and freeze. The dough can also be frozen after it has been shaped.

Pâté en croûte aux pistaches et abricots

PISTACHIO, APRICOT, AND PORK PIE

Across Lyon, the delis, butchers, and restaurants all claim to have designed the best *pâté en croûte*. This recipe brings together all my favorite elements for an ultimate—and easy—version.

Makes 1 loaf

Preparation time: 40 minutes

Resting time: 1 hour

Cooking time: 2 hours

Equipment: a Pullman loaf pan, lined with parchment

11½ oz/325 g lean ground pork

11½ oz/325 g veal or pork medallions, chopped finely but not minced

⅔ cup/100 g dried apricots or soft prunes, chopped into ¼-inch cubes

⅓ cup/50 g shelled pistachios, roughly chopped

Zest of ½ orange

Salt

½ tsp freshly ground black pepper

Generous pinch of freshly grated nutmeg

5½ tbsp/75 g butter

9 tbsp/125 g lard

5½ tbsp milk

⅓ cup hot water

3 cups/375 g all-purpose flour

1 egg yolk

Grainy mustard for serving

In a large bowl, mix together the pork, veal, apricots, pistachios, orange zest, ¼ tsp salt, pepper, and nutmeg. Cover the bowl with plastic wrap and refrigerate for 1 hour.

Place the butter, lard, 3½ tbsp of the milk, the water, and a pinch of salt in a saucepan over medium heat. Cook until the fats have melted, then remove the pan from the heat and let cool slightly. Pour the flour into a large bowl and make a well in the middle. Pour in the melted butter mixture and stir together. Shape the dough into a ball.

Set one-third of the dough aside. On a floured surface, roll out the other two-thirds of dough to an 8-by-10-inch rectangle about ¼ inch thick. Line the prepared pan with the dough, carefully pressing it into the corners and sides. Make sure there are no holes or cracks; fill them in with leftover pastry. Trim the excess pastry around the edges. Add the meat mixture and flatten it so it has a level surface and there are no gaps.

Preheat the oven to 350°F. Roll out the remainder of the pastry to a rectangle a little bigger than the top of the pan. Place the pastry on top of the filling and use a fork to press down and seal the edges. Mix the egg yolk with the remaining 2 tbsp milk to make an egg wash. Cut three little holes in the top of the pastry and brush the surface with the egg wash.

Wrap a small piece of foil around the handle of a wooden spoon to make a tube. Insert the tube into one of the holes, then repeat with the other holes. Cut a piece of foil the size of the top of your pie and make a slit in the middle. Cover the pie loosely, making sure that the vents stick out but the rest of the pastry is covered. Bake for 1½ hours, then remove the foil and bake for another 30 minutes until the crust is crisp and brown. Remove the pie from the oven and cool completely before loosening it from the pan. Slice and serve with grainy mustard.

La nouvelle salade Lyonnaise

NEW LYONNAIS SALAD

After a couple of days in Lyon, I was looking for some lighter fare. I came across Brazier Wine Bar, which has a fresh approach to French food, focusing more on using local seasonal produce than the classic meaty dishes of Lyon. The menu was short with only a couple of choices per course. A starter salad of smoked haddock and poached egg immediately caught my eye and was my inspiration for this main-course version, which features a few of my own additions.

Serves 4

Preparation time: 15 minutes
Cooking time: 15 minutes

Zest and juice of 1 lemon

4 tbsp extra-virgin olive oil

1 tbsp white wine vinegar

2 tbsp finely chopped chives

Pinch of sugar

4 sticks of celery, trimmed

1 small celeriac, peeled and very finely sliced

1 Granny Smith apple, unpeeled, cored and cubed

14 oz/400 g smoked haddock

2½ cups milk

4 fresh bay leaves

Generous pinch of freshly grated nutmeg

½ tsp white pepper

4 eggs

In a small bowl, whisk together the lemon zest and juice, olive oil, vinegar, chives, and sugar. Use a vegetable peeler to peel the celery into ribbons, then pat them dry with a paper towel. Toss the celeriac, apple, and celery with the oil mixture in a serving bowl.

Place the smoked haddock in a small saucepan with the milk, bay leaves, nutmeg, and pepper. The milk should completely cover the fish. Cover with a lid and cook over low heat for 6 minutes, or until the fish flakes apart when tested with a fork. Remove from the heat and set aside.

Bring a large pot of salted water to a boil over high heat. Pierce the larger end of each egg with a pin and gently lower into the hot water. When the water returns to a boil, lower the heat to a simmer, and begin timing. Allow 6 minutes for large eggs and 5 minutes for medium, then remove the eggs and run them under cold water. Peel the eggs.

Remove the fish from the milk with a slotted spoon. Peel off the skin and use a fork to flake the flesh into the bowl with the salad. Gently mix together the fish and salad before dividing between four serving plates and placing an egg on top of each salad. Drizzle with some of the poaching milk before serving.

Une petite astuce—tip Slicing the celeriac on a mandoline will make a world of difference to the texture.

Pizza Lyonnaise

LYONNAIS PIZZA

When I was a child, my mum was always trying to find clever ways to sneak offal into the family meal. Offal was, and still is, a cheap source of iron and protein, so Mum, ever one to watch the household budget, would make good use of these unfashionable offcuts. Lyon is famous for its use of offal, so I've taken a page out of Mum's book and mixed it up with a hint of ground beef for this pizza topping, making it taste slightly milder. Lots of zingy fresh flavors such as tomatoes, capers, red onion, and lemon zest vamp this up into such a treat that even my offal-loathing friends can't resist tucking in.

Makes 4 pizzas

Preparation time: 30 minutes
Cooking time: 20 minutes

5½ oz/150 g chicken or veal liver, kidneys, or heart (or a mixture), finely chopped

2 oz/50 g ground beef

1 red onion, finely chopped

3 tomatoes, finely chopped

2 cloves of garlic, crushed

2 tbsp capers, finely chopped

2 tbsp olive oil

1 tsp salt

3 sprigs of fresh thyme, leaves picked

1 tbsp finely chopped fresh rosemary

½ tsp cracked black pepper

1 recipe Pizza Dough (page 275)

2 tbsp finely chopped parsley

Zest of 1 lemon

Preheat the oven to 400°F. Line two large baking sheets with parchment. In a large bowl, combine the liver, beef, onion, tomatoes, garlic, capers, olive oil, salt, thyme, rosemary, and pepper.

Divide the dough into quarters and shape each piece into a ball. Dust the work surface lightly with flour and roll out the first ball to 10 inches in diameter and ¹⁄₁₆ inch thick. Place the dough on one of the sheets and spread with a quarter of the topping mix. Repeat with the remaining dough balls and topping so you have two pizzas to a sheet.

Bake for 20 minutes, or until the bottoms are crisp and lightly golden. Sprinkle with parsley and lemon zest just before serving.

Une petite astuce—tip If you're finding it hard to roll out the dough, use your hands to gently stretch it out.

Petits saucissons briochés

BABY BRIOCHE HOT DOGS

There are many culinary highlights from my trip to Lyon, but one of them has to be the *saucisson brioché*. The typical sausage to use is a *cervelas*, which is sometimes spiked with pistachio nuts or, on the higher end of the spectrum, stuffed with truffles AND pistachios. I tested out several sausages for this recipe, but the one that kept coming out on top was the classic hot dog sausage: the frankfurter or, as I know it, the wiener. Wiener sausages were often served at my Austrian grandma's table—not the cheap kind that disguise an array of artificial nastiness, but ones using good-quality meat, with a light smoky flavor. Of course, you can use any sausage you like; the key is quality and cooking time. And no hot dog is complete without a dollop of caramelized onion, or sauerkraut for an Alsatian twist.

Makes 8 hot dogs

Preparation time: 30 minutes
Resting time: 45 minutes
Cooking time: 40 minutes
Equipment: an 8-by-12-inch baking sheet, lined with parchment

2 tbsp butter

1 onion, finely sliced

Pinch of salt

Pinch of sugar

1 recipe brioche dough (see page 218), chilled for at least 2 hours

3 to 4 tbsp mustard (optional)

1 egg yolk

2 tbsp milk

4 frankfurters cut in half to make 8 shorter sausages

In a large sauté pan over medium-high heat, melt the butter. Add the onion, salt, and sugar and fry for about 10 minutes, until the onion is golden brown. Set aside.

On a lightly floured surface, roll out the brioche dough to a strip roughly 25 inches long and about 2 inches wider than the halved sausages.

Cut the dough into eight equal pieces and brush with the mustard (if using). Mix the egg yolk and the milk together to make an egg wash, then brush the egg wash along the edges of each dough rectangle. Place half a sausage in the middle of each rectangle and 1 tbsp of the caramelized onion on top of the sausage. Fold the dough over the sausage, making sure to overlap the edges and press down the ends to seal. Place the buns (seam-side down) on the baking sheet.

Brush the buns with egg wash and place in a warm place for about 45 minutes, until risen by 1 to 2 inches and puffy.

Preheat the oven to 350°F. Brush the buns a second time with egg wash and bake for 30 minutes, or until a skewer inserted into the middle comes out clean (cover the buns loosely with foil if they are browning too quickly).

Let cool for 5 minutes before turning out onto a wire rack. These are best eaten while still warm.

Croquettes

POTATO NUGGETS

On my travels around France, I always try to meet up with the locals. So it was great finding out that an old colleague, from the days when I worked at a Parisian department store, was from Lyon. I was lucky enough to catch up with Prudence and her mother over a cup of coffee. It was interesting to hear about the differences between the food cooked at home compared with the food eaten in the typical Lyonnais bouchons. Both speed and resourcefulness are key to home cooking, hence Prudence's mother's excellent idea for using up leftovers to make croquettes.

Makes about 18 nuggets

Preparation time: 15 minutes
Cooking time: 25 minutes

1¼ cups/250 g mashed potatoes

⅔ cup/100 g leftover cooked vegetables, cubed (carrots, parsnips, red pepper, peas); or finely chopped raw broccoli, mushrooms, ham, or roast meat; or grated hard cheese (Comté, Cheddar, or Gruyère)

Salt and freshly ground black pepper

4 tsp all-purpose flour

2 egg whites, beaten until light and foamy

½ cup/50 g breadcrumbs

2 tbsp sunflower or vegetable oil

Preheat the oven to 400°F.

In a medium bowl, mix together the mashed potatoes with your choice of leftovers until well combined. Season with salt and pepper and roll the mixture into small cylinders that will fit in the palm of your hand.

Set up three plates and one bowl in front of you. Dust one plate with the flour, pour the egg whites into the bowl, and spread the breadcrumbs on a second plate. Leave the third plate empty.

Roll the croquettes in the flour, dip them in the egg whites, and coat in the breadcrumbs. Place them on the clean plate.

Grease a rimmed baking sheet with the oil and heat in the oven for 10 minutes. Remove and carefully add all the croquettes. Bake for 10 minutes before flipping them and baking for 5 minutes more, until crispy and golden brown. Serve immediately.

Une petite astuce—tip Be sure to check the seasoning of the croquette mixture, as it will depend on the seasoning of your mash and leftovers.

Faire en avance—get ahead The croquettes can be made in advance and kept in an airtight container in the fridge for up to 2 days or frozen for up to 2 months.

Soupe à l'oignon et au reglisse avec des chips aux échalotes et fromage

ONION SOUP WITH SHALLOT-CHEESE CRISPS

Onion soup is one of the most warming and easiest dishes in the French culinary repertoire. Originally a poor man's dish made only with water and onions, a version including croûtons, beef stock, and caramelized onions appeared in the seventeenth century. In this recipe I've added my own twists with garlic and fennel for extra depth. Toss in some small pickled onions at the end if you'd like a little sharpness to cut through the richness.

Serves 4

Preparation time: 30 minutes
Cooking time: 1½ hours

3 tbsp/40 g butter

2 green onions, finely chopped, green parts reserved

2 large yellow onions, finely sliced

5 cloves of garlic, minced

1 tsp sugar

1 tsp fennel seeds

1⅔ cups dry white wine

6½ cups beef or vegetable stock

½ tsp Marmite (optional)

For the shallot-cheese crisps

8 shallots

4 thick slices of stale bread, cut into 1¼-inch cubes

1 tbsp melted butter

3 oz/80 g mature Comté, Beaufort, or other strongly flavored cheese, finely grated

Salt

12 small pickled onions (optional)

Melt the butter in a large saucepan over low heat and add the white parts of the green onions, the yellow onions, and garlic. Cook for about 45 minutes, stirring occasionally to make sure the garlic and onions don't stick to the bottom. When the onions are sticky, soft, and a deep golden color, sprinkle in the sugar and fennel seeds. Stir for a couple more minutes until the onions caramelize. Add the wine, stock, and Marmite (if using); cover; and simmer gently for 45 minutes.

Meanwhile, make the shallot-cheese crisps: Preheat the oven to 375°F and line a baking sheet with parchment. Peel and halve the shallots, then separate the layers to create shallot "leaves." Toss the leaves with the bread cubes and melted butter. Spread the cubes on the baking sheet. Sprinkle the cheese over the top and bake for 15 minutes, shaking the sheet occasionally. The cheese should be melted and slightly golden on the edges.

Taste the soup and add salt if needed. Ladle into serving bowls and top with the crisps. Sprinkle with the green parts of the green onion and the pickled onions, if desired. Serve immediately (the shallots go soggy in the soup).

Velouté de potimarron avec de la crème Chantilly, des oignons confits et des grains de potimarron

SILKY PUMPKIN SOUP WITH CREAM, ONION CONFIT, AND PUMPKIN SEEDS

Onion soup is pretty much a staple on every French alpine menu. But, listed just underneath, a vivacious orange pumpkin soup sometimes appears, looking almost out of place between the drabber winter fare. Roasting the pumpkin is well worth it as it takes on a rich sweetness; so much richer than being boiled in a pot of stock. The soup is delicious on its own, but add a little whipped cream sprinkled with some caramelized onions and crunchy seeds and you'll have a vibrant and colorful soup for dark winter days.

Serves 4

Preparation time: 30 minutes
Cooking time: 45 minutes

1 qt vegetable stock

2 lb/1 kg pumpkin or butternut squash, chopped into large pieces (reserve the seeds)

4 cloves of garlic, left whole and in their skins

2 tbsp olive oil

Salt

1 large onion, finely sliced

1 tbsp butter

Freshly ground pepper

½ cup whipping cream

Preheat the oven to 350°F.

In a medium saucepan, heat the stock. Arrange the pumpkin, garlic, and about half of the pumpkin seeds on a baking sheet. Toss with the oil and a pinch of salt. Roast for 30 minutes or until tender.

Let cool until you can handle the pumpkin, then scoop out the flesh into a pot. Discard the skin. Squeeze the garlic cloves from their skins and add to the pot.

Clean the seeds of any strands of pumpkin and place in a separate large sauté pan with the onion and butter. Fry over medium heat for about 10 minutes, stirring occasionally, until the onion begins to caramelize.

Meanwhile, finish the soup by adding the hot stock to the pumpkin and garlic. Blend the soup until smooth, using an immersion blender or puréeing in batches in a food processor or blender.Season with salt and pepper.

Whip the cream with a pinch of salt and plenty of black pepper. Ladle the soup into serving bowls and top with the whipped cream, caramelized onions, and pumpkin seeds.

Une petite astuce—tip If you're making this soup in advance, you may need to add a little extra stock when you reheat it, as the soup thickens when chilled.

Tourte à la saucisse et rognons

SMOKED SAUSAGE AND KIDNEY PIE

Meandering around Lyon, I saw butchers and delis accessorized with sausages strung up above the counters—smoked, cured, fresh, fat, or skinny. I couldn't resist a couple for the suitcase, although my clothes smelled of meat. Back in my little Paris kitchen, I thought that a Lyonnais twist on the British classic steak and kidney pie would be a great way to use my souvenirs.

Serves 4

Preparation time: 30 minutes
Cooking time: 1½ hours
Equipment: a pie plate about 8 inches round and 2½ inches deep

2 cups veal or beef stock

5½ oz/150 g smoked bacon, roughly chopped

7 oz/200 g smoked sausage, roughly chopped

6 shallots, halved

14 oz/400 g veal or lamb kidneys, trimmed of any sinew

2 cloves of garlic, peeled

4 new potatoes, washed

2 carrots, peeled and finely chopped

1 small cooked beet, peeled and roughly chopped

2 cups red wine

1 tbsp cornstarch

Salt and freshly ground pepper

1 egg, beaten

9 oz/250 g puff pastry

In a large saucepan over medium heat, warm the stock. In a separate large pot over medium-high heat, fry the bacon and smoked sausage. When the bacon begins to brown and release some of its fat, add the shallots, kidneys, and garlic and cook until the shallots are soft. Add the potatoes, carrots, beet, wine, and stock. Cover and simmer gently for 1 hour.

Using a slotted spoon, transfer all the meat and vegetables into the pie plate and pour the cooking liquid back into the saucepan.

Preheat the oven to 350°F.

Mix the cornstarch with water to make a slurry. Over medium heat, whisk the slurry into the stock. Continue to whisk until the stock has thickened to the consistency of heavy cream and started to bubble. Remove the stock from the heat and season with salt and pepper. Pour into the pie plate and brush the edge of the dish with the beaten egg.

Roll out the pastry to a thickness of ¼ inch and place on top of the pie plate. Press the pastry around the edge to seal. Use a knife to trim off any excess pastry, and cut a cross on the top. Brush the pastry twice with the beaten egg. Bake for 15 minutes, or until the pastry is golden and puffy. Cool for 10 minutes before serving. Leftovers will keep, refrigerated, for up to 2 days.

Une petite astuce—tip A good smoked sausage is essential to give the pie its delicious flavor.

Faire en avance—get ahead Make the filling a day or two in advance and refrigerate; it will allow the flavors to marry.

Crozets à la truite fumée et petits pois

BUCKWHEAT PASTA WITH SMOKED TROUT AND PEAS

The Savoie region has spectacular jade-green rivers and lakes, which are inhabited by brown and rainbow trout. Fishing for these prized fish is a popular pastime with locals and tourists alike, and it is well worth braving the glacier-cold waters to catch them, as the firm sweet flesh offers an excellent antidote to the heavy dishes associated with the region.

Serves 4

Preparation time: 25 minutes
Cooking time: 15 minutes

For the buckwheat pasta

1⅔ cups/200 g buckwheat flour

Pinch of salt

2 eggs

¼ cup milk

2 tbsp butter

1 onion, finely chopped

2 cloves of garlic, finely chopped

7 tbsp white wine

1 cup/150 g fresh or frozen peas

Heaping 2 tbsp crème fraîche

Freshly ground pepper

5½ oz/150 g smoked trout, cut into strips

4 radishes, thinly sliced, to garnish

2 tbsp trout or salmon roe (optional)

To make the buckwheat pasta: In a large bowl, mix the flour with the salt. Make a well in the middle, crack in the eggs, and add the milk. Stir together until you get a lump of dough.

Dust the work surface with plenty of flour and divide the dough in half. Take one half and dust it with more flour. Roll it out to a thickness of about ⅟₁₆ inch, then cut into very small diamond shapes (about ¼ inch). Slide a plastic pastry scraper under the pasta to lift it off the surface. Toss it gently to break it up and place it on a lightly dusted baking sheet. Roll out the second half of the dough and repeat.

Bring a large pot of salted water to a boil.

Meanwhile, place the butter, onion, and garlic in a large pan over medium heat. Cook for 3 to 4 minutes, until the onion has softened. Add the wine and simmer while you cook the pasta.

When the water has come to a boil, add the peas and pasta. When the pasta floats to the top (roughly 2 minutes), use a slotted spoon to transfer the peas and pasta to the pan with the onion. Stir in the crème fraîche and season with pepper. Remove the pan from the heat before gently mixing in the smoked trout and garnishing with the radishes and trout roe (if using). Serve immediately.

Salade Savoyarde avec une vinaigrette de noix

CHUNKY SAVOIE SALAD WITH A WALNUT VINAIGRETTE

I love a good salad, especially in the French style, known as *gourmande*. This word has no literal English translation, but it evokes gastronomic indulgence and pleasure. Each region in France has its own version of this salad, to showcase the area's ingredients, whether a local ham, a cheese, or a variety of bean. After a few days of skiing in the French Alps, the crunchy raw textures were a welcome break from the rich foods I had been savoring. The version I had was a well-dressed green salad (a good vinaigrette is essential) enriched with lardons and Beaufort cheese. Back at home I re-created the flavors, souping-up the salad with a few extras: walnuts, apple, and some peppery radishes for sweetness and bite. Switch and mix up the vegetables to your own taste and based on what's in season.

Serves 4 as a main course, or 8 as a side

Preparation time: 20 minutes
Cooking time: 10 minutes

½ cup/50 g walnuts

3½ tbsp sunflower oil

2 tbsp white wine vinegar

Pinch of salt

1 small head of leafy lettuce, washed, dried, and roughly torn

10 radishes, thinly sliced

1 apple, cubed

1 small cucumber, cut in ribbons

4 strips of bacon

2 thick slices of bread, cut into ¾-inch squares

3½ oz/100 g Beaufort or other strongly flavored cheese, shaved

Salt and freshly ground black pepper

Crusty bread to serve

In a small sauté pan over medium heat, toast the walnuts. Chop them finely and combine with the oil, vinegar, and salt in a large serving bowl. Add the lettuce, radishes, apple, and cucumber to the vinaigrette and toss.

In a large sauté pan over medium heat, fry the bacon and bread until golden. Sprinkle the mixture on top of the salad along with the cheese. Toss together and season with salt and pepper. Serve immediately with some crusty bread.

Une petite astuce—tip Walnuts can be replaced with other nuts such as pine nuts, pecans, or hazelnuts.

Haricots savoyard avec lentilles aux herbes

GREEN BEAN BUNDLES WITH HERB LENTIL SALAD

In France, one way of spotting a good bistro is by the standard of their *haricots verts*. Spot a dull, limp green bean and it's either come from a can or has been overcooked; rarely the sign of a good chef at work. Wrap anything in *jambon de Savoie* (a smoky ham) and add a regional cheese, such as Beaufort, and you'll have the essence of the flavors of Savoie at your fingertips. Traditionally, veal is stuffed with Beaufort cheese and wrapped in smoky ham, but green beans work just as well.

Serves 4 to 6
Preparation time: 20 minutes
Cooking time: 30 minutes

14 oz/400 g fresh green beans, trimmed

3½ oz/100 g Beaufort or other strongly flavored hard cheese, cut into thin sticks the length of a green bean

8 slices of smoky ham, speck, or Parma ham

1 cup/200 g Puy lentils

1 bay leaf

1 onion, finely chopped

1 tbsp butter

2 sprigs of thyme, leaves only

1 tbsp grainy mustard

Preheat the oven to 350°F. Bring a large pot of salted water to a boil. Add the green beans and boil for 4 minutes, or until the beans are cooked but still crunchy. Remove the beans (you can keep the water for boiling the lentils) and run under cold water to stop the cooking.

Take about ten beans, add a couple sticks of cheese, and wrap a slice of ham tightly around the middle to keep everything together. Place in a baking dish and repeat with the rest of the beans, cheese, and ham. Bake for 20 minutes, or until the ham begins to crisp.

Meanwhile, bring the water back to a boil. Add the lentils and bay leaf. Cook for 15 to 20 minutes, or until the lentils are al dente. Drain and run under cold water to stop the cooking.

In a medium sauté pan over medium heat, fry the onion with the butter and thyme until soft and translucent. Add the lentils and mustard and stir. Remove the lentils from the heat, and serve immediately with the green bean bundles.

Les petits pains au fromage fondu avec une salade de chouxfleur et cornichons

BREAD ROLL FONDUES WITH CAULIFLOWER SALAD

A trip to the French Alps wouldn't be complete without a pot of fondue. The combination and ratio of cheeses always varies, with each cook boasting their own secret recipe. In general, it's a mix of a local strong cheese, like Beaufort, mellowed out by a milder cheese like Emmental. The classic fondue uses a fondue pot complete with burner, but, unfortunately, there just isn't room for any more kitchen gadgets in my little Paris kitchen, so I came up with an alternative solution. Bread rolls make for the perfect edible pots and offer your guests a warm, golden, oozy surprise. If you like, substitute romanesco for cauliflower.

Serves 6
Preparation time: 15 minutes
Cooking time: 10 to 15 minutes

1 small head of cauliflower, broken into florets

2 tbsp white wine vinegar

1 tbsp grainy mustard

2 tbsp sunflower oil

15 cornichons, roughly chopped

10 small pickled onions, roughly chopped

Salt

6 medium bread rolls

1 clove of garlic, peeled

½ cup dry white wine

1 tsp lemon juice

5½ oz/150 g Beaufort, Gruyère, or mature Cheddar, finely grated

3½ oz/100 g Emmental, finely grated

Preheat the oven to 350°F. Bring a large pot of water to a boil. Add the cauliflower and cook for 4 minutes, or until the cauliflower is cooked but still crunchy. Drain and run under cold water to stop the cooking.

In a large bowl, combine the vinegar, mustard, and oil. Add the cauliflower, cornichons, and pickled onions and toss in the dressing. Season with salt, then set aside.

Place the bread rolls in the oven and, while they crisp up, make a fondue. Rub the inside of a small saucepan with the garlic clove. Add the wine and lemon juice and bring to a boil. Turn the heat to low and stir in the Beaufort and Emmental until completely melted. When you have a runny sauce, remove the rolls from the oven. Slice the top off each roll and use your thumb to press down the dough in the middle to create a hollow. Fill with the cheesy sauce and replace the bread lid. Serve immediately with the salad on the side.

Les oeufs au chocolat

CHOCOLATE EGGS

Pâques (Easter) is the ultimate occasion for *pâtissiers* to flex their chocolate-making skills. The French like to celebrate with a broad range of chocolate surprises: from cocoa fish and monkeys to tree trunks and milkmaid figurines. Traditional themes and simple egg shapes are for amateurs. A bit of a traditionalist, however, I remain fond of a good, old Easter egg, especially little ones filled with praline.

Makes 6 eggs

Preparation time: 20 minutes

Cooking time: 15 minutes

Setting time: 3 hours

Equipment: a piping bag wih a small nozzle; six 16-inch lengths of ribbon, ½ to ¾ inch wide

6 eggs

9 oz/255 g dark chocolate, finely chopped

1 tsp sunflower oil

½ cup/50 g chopped Praline (page 276), or finely chopped pistachios, dehydrated strawberries, or raspberries

¾ cup plus 1 tbsp heavy cream

2 tbsp butter, softened

Preheat the oven to 325°F. Use a needle or metal skewer to poke a hole in the bottom of one of the eggs (on the nonpointy side). Wiggle the needle until the hole is ⅜ inch wide. Poke a tiny hole in the opposite end. Blow through the tiny hole to push the egg out through the larger hole and into a bowl. Repeat with the rest of the eggs. Reserve the eggs for another use.

Rinse out the egg shells. Place them on a baking sheet and bake 10 minutes to sterilize them. Cool completely before using.

Melt 2 oz/55 g of the chocolate in a heatproof bowl placed over a saucepan of gently simmering water (don't let the base of the bowl touch the water). Stir occasionally, until melted, then stir in the oil. Pour 1 tsp of the melted chocolate into one of the egg-shells. Swirl it around and then turn it upside down and leave it to drain in an old egg carton. Repeat with the rest of the eggs.

Make a second layer of chocolate inside each egg, but before leaving it to set, drop 1 tsp of the chopped praline inside each one and shake it around so it sticks to the chocolate. Repeat with the rest of the eggs and praline. Refrigerate to set for 30 minutes.

Place the remaining 7 oz/200 g of chocolate in a heatproof bowl. Bring the cream just to a boil in a saucepan and pour over the chocolate. Leave for 2 minutes and then stir and add the butter. Pour the ganache into the piping bag and pipe into the eggs through the larger hole. Shake the egg to release any air bubbles, then place in an egg carton at room temperature for several hours, or refrigerate for 30 minutes to set. Wrap a ribbon around each egg to cover the hole at the bottom before serving.

Tarte au chocolat et crème fraîche

CHOCOLATE AND CRÈME FRAÎCHE TART

Bernachon, a chocolate shop in Lyon, selects its own cocoa beans, then roasts and grinds them together to create a unique blend. If you're ever in Lyon, be sure to stop in, even if it is just to *lèche la vitrine* (lick the window), as the French aptly describe window-shopping. One of their chocolate blends—the *Palais d'Or* (Golden Palace), made with crème fraîche—happens to translate equally well into a rich and luxurious tart.

Serves 12

Preparation time: 30 minutes
Resting time: 2½ hours
Cooking time: 45 minutes
Equipment: a 9-inch round tart pan, at least 1 inch deep

2 tbsp butter

1 recipe Sweet Pastry Dough (page 275)

7½ oz/215 g dark chocolate, finely chopped

2 oz/55 g milk chocolate, finely chopped

1 cup crème fraîche

3½ tbsp milk

Pinch of salt

4 oz/115 g white chocolate

1 tbsp coconut oil

Grease the tart pan with the butter. Preheat the oven to 350°F. Roll out the dough between two sheets of parchment until it is ⅛ to ¼ inch thick.

Line the prepared pan with the pastry dough, trimming away any excess, and prick the base several times with a fork. Place a sheet of parchment on top and pour in pie weights. Bake for 20 minutes before removing the weights and parchment. Bake for 10 minutes more, then remove from the oven and let cool.

Put 5½ oz/155 g of the dark chocolate, all the milk chocolate, the crème fraîche, milk, and salt in a heatproof bowl and place it over a pan of gently simmering water (don't let the base of the bowl touch the water). Stir occasionally until melted. Pour the chocolate into the cooked and cooled tart shell. Refrigerate for 1½ hours to set.

In the meantime, melt the remaining dark chocolate in a heatproof bowl over a pan of gently simmering water, as before. When melted, pour the chocolate onto a large piece of parchment and spread thin using a spatula. Refrigerate until set, then snap the chocolate into 2-inch shards. Repeat with the white chocolate, adding the coconut oil as the chocolate melts.

When the tart has chilled, remove it from the fridge and jab the shards into the surface of the filling. If you're not serving immediately, remove it from the fridge anyway and keep it in a cool, dark place. The tart is best eaten at room temperature, but keeps, refrigerated, for up to 3 days.

Brioche

As a child I would eat brioche like it was going out of fashion. There's something so satisfying about the texture: doughy like bread, sweet like cake, and positioned somewhere between naughty and normal. It's unsurprising really; it's essentially a bread pumped up with plenty of butter, eggs, and a hit of sweetness.

Makes 1 loaf

Preparation time: 30 minutes using the mixer; 45 minutes by hand (be prepared for a workout)
Resting time: 2¾ hours, or overnight
Cooking time: 30 minutes
Equipment: a Pullman loaf pan, lined with parchment

2 cups/240 g bread flour

2 tbsp superfine sugar

1 tsp salt

Scant 2 tsp instant yeast

6½ tbsp milk

2 eggs, plus 2 egg yolks

1½ cups/125 g butter, cubed and softened

Small handful of coarse or pearl sugar

Place the flour, superfine sugar, salt, and yeast in the bowl of a stand mixer fitted with the dough hook. On slow speed, combine the dry ingredients, then add 4½ tbsp of the milk, the eggs, and 1 egg yolk and continue to mix on slow speed for 2 minutes. Increase the speed to medium for 6 to 8 minutes more. The dough will become soft, smooth, and elastic.

Add the softened butter one cube at a time. Continue to mix until the butter is thoroughly combined (roughly another 5 minutes). Scrape the bowl down periodically with a spatula to ensure all the butter is incorporated. Cover with plastic wrap and chill the dough for at least 2 hours, or overnight.

Lightly dust the work surface and your hands with flour. Pour out the dough and knead for 1 minute before forming into a sausage shape that fits into the loaf pan. Whisk together the remaining 2 tbsp milk and remaining egg yolk to make an egg wash. Pop the dough into the prepared pan, seam-side down, and brush with the egg wash. Let the dough rise in a warm place for 45 minutes, or until it doubles in size. Do not leave it anywhere too hot, as the butter in the brioche will start to melt.

Preheat the oven to 350°F. Brush the brioche with more egg wash and sprinkle with the coarse sugar. Bake for 30 minutes, or until a skewer inserted into the middle comes out clean. Cover the brioche with foil if it's browning too quickly.

Remove the brioche from the oven and let cool for 5 minutes before removing from the pan and placing on a wire rack to cool completely. The brioche will keep, tightly wrapped, at room temperature, for up to 3 days.

Brioche à la praline

PRALINE BRIOCHE

Bright pink, sugar-coated almonds are the star ingredient in Lyonnais pâtisserie. Unlike classic praline, Lyonnais praline is not caramelized. Instead, the sugar is heated and left snow white, then dyed bright pink. Lyonnais praline is sold in packets and can be eaten on its own, but often it is spotted on tarts, cakes, and desserts. I think the best way of eating it is when paired with a soft, buttery brioche. This recipe makes double the amount of praline needed for the brioche, in case you subscribe to my method of cooking, which involves a lot of tasting along the way. You can store the rest in an airtight container for up to 3 months.

Makes 1 loaf

Preparation time: 30 minutes using the mixer, 45 minutes by hand

Resting time: 45 minutes

Cooking time: 45 minutes

Equipment: a Pullman loaf pan, lined with parchment; candy thermometer

⅓ cup water

2 cups/400 g sugar

⅔ cup/100 g blanched almonds

Good-quality red gel food coloring (see Tip, page 221)

1 recipe Brioche dough (see facing page), chilled for at least 2 hours

1 egg yolk

2 tbsp milk

Line a baking sheet with parchment. Pour half the water into a medium saucepan over medium heat with half the sugar and bring to a boil. Don't stir, but gently swirl the pan until the sugar dissolves. When it reaches 275°F (the hard-ball stage) on the candy thermometer, remove it from the heat and stir in half the almonds. Continue to stir until the sugar has a sandy texture. Pour the mixture onto the prepared baking sheet to cool. Pick out and discard any lumps of sugar.

When the almonds are almost cool, bring the remaining water and sugar along with the food coloring to 275°F. Quickly stir in the nuts so they are coated in the sugar and then immediately tip them back out onto the baking sheet. Too much stirring will make the sugar sandy, but do make sure each almond is coated individually in the pink sugar. Let cool before roughly chopping 3½ oz/100 g (and storing the rest in an airtight container).

Remove the brioche dough from the fridge. Dust the work surface and the top of the dough with flour, then roll out to a square, roughly 16 by 16 inches. Move the dough around from time to time to make sure it's not sticking to the work surface (dust with more flour if needed).

continued

Whisk together the egg yolk and milk to make an egg wash. Cut the dough into 6 equal squares. Brush each one with egg wash and sprinkle with the chopped praline (keep a little for sprinkling at the end). Lay the squares loosely against one another in the lined loaf pan, slotting them side by side like books on a shelf, filling the pan two-thirds full. You might find it easier with the pan on its side.

Brush the dough with egg wash and let rise in a warm (but not too hot) place for 45 minutes, or until it has risen by 1 or 2 inches and looks puffy.

Preheat the oven to 350°F. Carefully brush the brioche with egg wash and sprinkle with the remaining praline. Bake for 30 minutes, or until a skewer inserted into the middle comes out clean. Let cool for 5 minutes before turning out onto a wire rack to cool completely. The brioche will keep, tightly wrapped, at room temperature, for up to 3 days.

Les petites astuces—tips Avoid buying the cheap liquid food coloring, as it usually takes a whole bottle to get a decent color. If you can't find the gel, then use a colored powder.

Cover the brioche with a piece of foil if it's browning too quickly.

Tarte aux noix, sarrasin et caramel salé

WALNUT AND BUCKWHEAT CARAMEL TART

Grenoble is known not only for being the capital of the Alps, but also for its walnuts, which were awarded with an AOC label, making them the most sought after in France. When the season arrives, the vegetable man at my local market in Paris will have a box of them for sale. I am not going to lie, they are a bit of a pain to crack open—but luckily it's possible to buy them already shelled. Walnuts have a slight bitter note that works particularly well with sweet and salty caramel, and the toasted buckwheat grains add additional crunch.

Makes 1 tart

Preparation time: 30 minutes
Cooking time: 45 minutes
Equipment: a 4½-by-14-inch tart pan; kitchen thermometer

1 recipe Shortcrust Pastry Dough (page 274)

¾ cup/150 g sugar

2 tbsp water

7 tbsp heavy cream

2 tbsp golden syrup or molasses

3 tbsp butter

½ tsp salt

2½ cups/250 g walnuts, toasted

1 cup/150 g buckwheat, toasted

Grease the tart pan. Preheat the oven to 350°F. Roll out the dough between two sheets of parchment until ⅛ to ¼ inch thick.

Line the pan with the pastry and prick the base several times with a fork. Place a sheet of parchment on top and pour in pie weights. Bake for 20 minutes before removing the parchment and weights. Bake for 10 minutes more. Remove from the oven and let cool slightly before removing the pastry shell from the pan.

Put half the sugar in a large saucepan with the water. Place the saucepan over high heat and allow the sugar to melt. Do not stir, but swirl the pot around if needed. Once the caramel becomes a dark reddish-brown, remove it from the heat and add the cream, golden syrup, butter, and salt. Be careful: the caramel will steam and bubble. Swirl the pan before returning it to medium heat. Cook the caramel for 3 to 4 minutes, or until it reaches 235°F on the kitchen thermometer.

Stir in the walnuts and buckwheat and then pour immediately into the tart shell. Spread out the filling and leave for 10 minutes to set at room temperature before serving.

Alsace

LE BRETZEL

LE KOUGELHOPF

LE CHRISTKINDELSMÄRIK

LES KNACKS

LA TERRINE BAECKEOFFE

ALSACE

STRASBOURG

ALLEMAGNE

LA WINSTUB

LES MAENNELES

LA FACHWARIKHÜS

LES VOSGES

LA ROUTE DU VIN D'ALSACE

COLMAR

RHIN

LE COSTUME ALSACIEN

LES BREDELES

MULHOUSE

SUISSE

LE GEWÜRZTRAMINER

LE FROMAGE BLANC

LA BIERE

LA CHOUCROUTE

LE STORCK

CINNAMON SPICE, FESTIVE DELIGHTS, AND LOTS OF ICE

Perhaps it was the wood-beamed architecture, love of sausage, and wafting smells of sweet spiced cakes that meant Alsace, out of all the regions I visited, felt the most familiar to me, even though I had never visited it before.

Alsace lies in the northeastern corner of France, with Germany bordering to the north and east, and Switzerland to the south. Its location has resulted in a unique blend of cultures, drawing influences from all its neighbors, especially Germany. I had eaten some of the typical Alsatian cuisine, like sauerkraut with smoked sausage—its most famous export. Many other dishes, such as spätzle, *kugelhopf*, and *bredele*, used flavors I recognized from spending my teenage years in Bavaria.

I headed to Alsace a week before Christmas and it turned out to be the busiest time of the year to visit, with the famous Christmas markets in full swing. The air was filled with a heady mix of *vin chaud aux épices* (mulled spiced wine), candied nuts, and pine needles. Christmas trees and twigs decorated the outside of little wooden huts, delicately draped with bright twinkling lights.

When evening descends, the markets truly come to life, with people sipping hot mulled wine and munching on sausages, *bretzel*, or some of the many sweet treats on offer, including waffles, crêpes, and a wonderful array of Christmas cookies. In Strasbourg, the region's capital, I found a market that had a handful of stands run by local producers. One was selling goat cheese, another showcasing artisanal beer; a local mushroom grower offered a selection of dried and fresh mushrooms, and a flour miller artisanal flours and cookies. . . . All of them were warm and welcoming in spite of the finger-numbing cold (wrapping your hands around a warm cup of *vin chaud* is a must at all times).

Luckily, the action doesn't just take place outside. There's plenty to discover inside too. The Alsatians have their version of a bistro, the *winstub*, although it is a little less grand than the ones you see in Paris. Think wooden chairs with little hearts carved out in the back, red-and-white checked tablecloths, and a heartwarming atmosphere. Portions are generous, definitely not for the fainthearted. *Choucroute garnie*, *baeckehoffe* (see page 247), and *flammekueche*, a sort of pizza made with crème fraîche, onion, and bacon, are never off the menu, no matter whether it's freezing cold outside or the height of summer. The bakeries are delightful, with the famous *kugelhopf* in various sizes on display; around Christmastime most of them will bring out an amazing assortment of biscuits. Chocolate shops are crammed with goodies, like confit-covered chestnuts and plenty of marzipan figures.

If sweets aren't your thing, make sure to pop by a butcher (I recommend Frick Lutz in Strasbourg) for a huge selection of cold meats and sausages. What we would see as a frankfurter or hot dog is something of a specialty here. But do not think that all hot dogs are the same; there's a reason why the locals call them *"le knack"*: a good one will snap loudly. With your sausage you'll need some beer, of course. Alsatians love their beer, and there are plenty of brasseries in which to drink a pint or two (I even found one in Strasbourg, microbrasserie La Lanterne, that brewed its own).

Despite the damage caused by the bombing during the Second World War, most of the cities and towns in the area have managed to keep their original architecture: buildings with exposed wooden beams and shutters painted in pastel colors, and, during the summer months, window boxes planted with colorful flowers flowing over the sides. Colmar is particularly renowned for its picturesque architecture, making it a popular destination for busloads of tourists. It's almost Disney-esque and a bit too perfect for my liking, but still well worth a visit.

As you head out of the urban areas toward the mountains, nature takes over. Buildings become a little more "lived in" and rural. *Le route du vin*, an attraction just as famous as the Christmas markets, runs from the north to the south of Alsace and celebrates the region's long winemaking tradition, which dates back to when the Romans invaded Alsace and made it their center of viticulture. Some of the famous local wines include Riesling, Gewürztraminer, Sylvaners, and Muscat.

Alsace had me utterly charmed. Deciding what recipes to feature, twist, or simply convey in their classic form for this chapter was far from an easy task. I decided to include some aromatic edible gifts; both a classic *kugelhopf* and one with a savory twist (see pages 254 and 258); a hearty glazed ham hock for sharing with friends in the cold months (see page 241); and cute little coconut snowballs inspired by the winter weather (see page 265).

Knepfles à l'épeautre avec Munster et feuilles d'oignons

BUTTON DUMPLINGS WITH MUNSTER CHEESE AND ONION PETALS

Not far from Strasbourg, the capital of Alsace, lies the Moulin de Hurtigheim, a small family-run flour mill and one of the last independently owned mills in the region. It was fascinating to learn about the different grains used to produce particular flours, and see the flour truck that goes around the villages selling flour directly to locals. This dish has its origins in the German word for "small button" and, although these tiny dumplings can be made with regular white flour, I find spelt adds a certain nuttiness. It's perfect with sweet onions and the local Munster cheese, or equally delicious served with a pasta sauce or in a soup.

Serves 2 as a main course
Preparation time: 25 minutes
Resting time: 30 minutes
Cooking time: 30 minutes
Equipment: a piping bag with a ½-inch nozzle

1 cup/125 g spelt flour

½ tsp salt

1 egg, beaten

½ cup/125 g fromage blanc or quark

1 red onion

1 tbsp butter

1 tbsp brown sugar

2 tbsp red wine vinegar

Salt and freshly ground pepper

2 oz/50 g Munster cheese, sliced, or other strongly flavored soft cheese, such as Camembert or Brie

In a bowl, mix together the spelt and salt in a bowl and make a well in the middle. Pour in the beaten egg and fromage blanc and mix together until you have a smooth dough. Place the dough in the piping bag.

Line a baking sheet with parchment and pipe thick lines of dough across the paper. Place the sheet of piped dough in the freezer for 30 minutes.

In the meantime, preheat the oven to 400°F and line a baking sheet with foil. Peel the onion, then halve lengthwise and trim the root. Cut each half into thirds lengthwise. Carefully pull away the individual layers of the onion right up to the heart; you will be left with lots of little onion petals. Add them to the baking sheet; toss with the butter, brown sugar, and vinegar; and season with salt and pepper. Cook in the oven for 30 minutes.

Remove the sheet from the freezer and cut the dough strips into ¼-inch rectangles to make your *knepfles*. A knife dipped in hot water may help.

Bring a large pot of water to a boil over high heat. Drop the *knepfles* into the boiling water; when they float to the top, they are cooked. Drain in a colander and toss with the red onion leaves. Top with a layer of cheese and serve immediately.

Strasbourg

Frites Alsaciennes au bibelaskäs

ALSATIAN OVEN FRIES WITH FROMAGE BLANC

When I visited my first traditional Alsatian restaurant, I had a serious case of food envy. Despite how delicious my *bouchée à la reine* (see page 233) was, I couldn't resist pinching some of my dining partner Marie's *bibelaskäs*—a luscious fresh cheese like fromage blanc. It had several accompaniments on the side: finely chopped shallots, little green onion rounds, and clusters of chopped aromatic herbs. A pile of hot and crunchy potatoes quickly followed, presenting themselves as perfect dunking devices. Luckily, Marie was kind enough to share her recipe for this lighter version of cheesy chips, a recipe that combines her loves for her hometown of Strasbourg and her new home, New York City.

Serves 4

Preparation time: 15 minutes
Cooking time: 20 minutes

2¼ lb/1 kg potatoes

4 tbsp olive oil

Salt

2 cups/500 g fromage blanc or quark

Freshly ground black pepper

1 small bunch of chives,
finely chopped

2 shallots, finely chopped

2 small green onions, finely chopped

1 small bunch of flat-leaf parsley,
finely chopped

1 small bunch of cilantro,
finely chopped

Preheat the oven to 400°F. Wash and dry the potatoes. Cut them lengthwise into slim ⅜-inch batons, leaving the skin on, and then place in a large saucepan of cold water. Bring the water to a boil over medium heat. As soon as the water starts boiling, cook the fries for exactly 1 minute. Drain the fries through a colander. They should still be uncooked and firm to the touch at this point. Place a kitchen towel on a large cutting board, arrange the fries on top, and blot them dry.

Line a baking sheet with parchment. Tip the fries onto the parchment, pour the oil on top, and mix to coat. Season with salt, then spread them out in a single layer. Bake for 20 minutes, checking on them after 10 minutes, and turning them over so they brown evenly.

Divide the fromage blanc between four small bowls and season with salt and pepper. When the fries come out of the oven, season them with salt and sprinkle with the chopped chives. Divide between the four bowls.

Place bowls of the shallots, green onions, parsley, and cilantro on the table, along with the bowls of cheese and fries for everyone to help themselves.

Bouchées à la reine végétarienne

VEGETABLE PASTRY PUFFS

During lunch at a cozy *winstub*, I spotted a dish at a neighboring table and immediately knew it was the one for me. It was a golden puff-pastry frame, filled with dumplings, chicken, and a creamy sauce. After a week in hearty and carnivorous Alsace, I arrived back at my little Paris kitchen craving vegetables, and so I decided to swap the meat for some vibrant green broccoli and cauliflower. If you like, you can replace some of the vegetables with leftover roast chicken.

Serves 4
Preparation time: 15 minutes
Cooking time: 35 minutes

1⅔ cups vegetable stock

13 oz/375 g puff pastry,
at room temperature

1 egg

2 tbsp milk

3 cups/200 g broccoli florets

3 cups/200 g cauliflower florets

2 tbsp butter

¼ cup/30 g all-purpose flour

Zest of ½ lemon

7 tbsp Riesling or other dry white wine

4 tbsp heavy cream

1 tsp lemon juice

Pinch of sugar

Salt and freshly ground black pepper

In a medium saucepan over medium heat, warm the stock. Preheat the oven to 350°F. Line a baking sheet with parchment. Roll out the puff pastry between two sheets of parchment to a thickness of ¼ inch. Using a sharp knife, cut the pastry into four rectangles, each about 5 by 4 inches. Place the pastry pieces on the baking sheet, leaving a little space between each one. Whisk together the egg and milk to make an egg wash. Using a knife, lightly score a border ½ inch in from the edge. Brush the pastry with egg wash and bake for 15 minutes, until golden brown.

Meanwhile, steam the broccoli and cauliflower florets until just tender. Remove the pastry from the oven, gently cut along the scored border, and pull out a few layers from the inside to create room for the filling.

Melt the butter in a large saucepan over medium heat. Add the flour and beat until you have a smooth paste. Continue to beat until the roux begins to turn golden. Remove the pan from the heat and gradually add the hot stock and lemon zest, whisking constantly.

Return the pan to medium heat and simmer gently for 10 minutes, whisking frequently to ensure the sauce doesn't stick to the bottom of the pan. (If the sauce becomes too thick, whisk in a little more stock or water.)

Add the wine and simmer for 10 minutes more, then remove the pan from the heat and whisk in the cream, lemon juice, and sugar. Season with salt and pepper. Add the vegetables to the pastry *bouchée* and ladle over plenty of the sauce. Serve immediately.

Crackers aux grains de carvi et pomme

CARAWAY AND APPLE CRACKERS

The influence of nearby Germany has introduced darker, more wholesome flours to the Alsace region, like rye and whole wheat. Rye flour marries beautifully with caraway—another local favorite—so I've brought the two together in these rustic crackers. A hint of apple adds a welcome sweetness. Be warned, these aren't your average cardboard crackers; I could easily munch my way through a batch of these fresh from the oven. If they make it past the fresh-out-of-the-oven munching stage, try serving these on a cheese board.

Makes 8 large crackers (with off-cuts)

Preparation time: 15 minutes
Resting time: 1 hour
Cooking time: 20 minutes
Equipment: a small heart-shaped cookie cutter (optional)

1¾ cups/200 g rye flour

½ tbsp caraway seeds

1 tsp instant yeast

½ tsp salt

Pinch of sugar

1 Granny Smith apple, unpeeled, cored and roughly grated

⅓ cup warm water

In a large bowl, mix together the rye flour, caraway seeds, yeast, salt, sugar, and apple. Pour in the water and mix until you have a sticky ball. Cover the bowl with a clean wet tea towel and leave to rest in a warm place for 1 hour.

Preheat the oven to 350°F. Line two baking sheets with parchment. Dust the work surface with rye flour.

Divide the dough in half and roll out one half to a thickness of about ⅛ inch (you may need to dust the dough with flour if it is a bit sticky).

Cut the dough into rectangles, roughly 5 by 3½ inches. If you like, cut out the center of each one with the cookie cutter to make them look like the shutters on traditional Alsatian houses. Use a brush to dust off any excess flour, then place the dough on the baking sheets. Repeat with the other half of the dough.

Bake for 20 minutes, or until the crackers are crisp. If cooking the cut-out hearts as well, these will only take a couple of minutes. Leave to cool on a wire rack. The crackers will keep in an airtight container for several weeks.

Les petites astuces—tips The caraway seeds can be omitted or replaced with other seeds like poppy or sunflower.

A pear would work well instead of the apple, or even a very thinly sliced red onion.

Pad Alsacien

ALSATIAN NOODLES

Alsatian food is hearty fare, so I soon found myself craving something crunchy and fresh. Alsatian egg noodles reminded me of those used in the classic Thai street food dish, pad Thai. And so, using local ingredients, the *pad Alsacien* was born. Cabbage and carrots add the crunch, lardons provide some lip-smacking saltiness, and, for heat, I've used freshly grated horseradish.

Serves 4

Preparation time: 15 minutes
Cooking time: 10 minutes

4 tbsp/85 g runny honey

6 tbsp white wine vinegar

Salt

10½ oz/300 g Alsatian flat noodles or other flat egg noodles

2 tbsp sunflower oil

7 oz/200 g smoked bacon, cubed

2 carrots, peeled and cut into matchsticks

¼ head red cabbage, halved, cored, and finely sliced

7 oz/200 g mushrooms, wiped and quartered

4 shallots, finely sliced

4 cloves of garlic, finely chopped

2 green onions, white and green parts separated, finely sliced

Heaping 2 tbsp finely grated fresh horseradish

In a small bowl, stir together the honey and vinegar and season with salt. Set aside.

Bring a large pot of water to a boil over high heat and cook the noodles until al dente. Drain, setting aside a little of the cooking liquid.

Heat the oil in a wok or large frying pan over high heat until smoking. Add the bacon, carrots, cabbage, mushrooms, and noodles. Stir-fry for 2 minutes. Add the shallots, garlic, and the white parts of the green onions. Fry for 2 minutes more before adding the honey sauce and 2 to 3 tbsp of the pasta liquid. Turn off the heat and mix in the horseradish. Serve immediately, with the green parts of the green onion sprinkled on top.

Les petites astuces—tips You can use almost any vegetable you have in the fridge: bell peppers, zucchini, eggplants, broccoli . . . just make sure to cut them finely, so they cook quickly.

If you can't find fresh horseradish, use 1 tbsp jarred grated horseradish.

Jambonneau à la bière

BEER-BRAISED HAM HOCK

Alsace is not only the land of Gewürztraminer, Riesling, and Grüner Veltliner wines, it's also famous for another alcoholic offering: beer. While I hardly need to state the merits of drinking beer, it also does a good job of tenderizing meat. The Alsatian love of beer and pork is showcased in this popular brasserie dish.

Serves 4 to 6

Preparation time: 10 to 15 minutes
Resting time: 2 hours, or overnight
Cooking time: 3½ to 4 hours

2 ham hocks (each weighing about 2½ lb/1.2 kg) or 4 small ones (see Tip)

6 cups pale beer

6 cups water

Salt

Zest of 1 lemon, plus 2 tbsp lemon juice

10 black peppercorns

4 tbsp/85 g runny honey

4 tbsp/60 g Dijon mustard

2 onions, quartered

4 carrots, peeled and sliced lengthwise

1 stick of celery, cut in half

1¼ cups/250 g Puy or green lentils

1 small bunch parsley, leaves only, finely chopped

Score the skin of the ham hocks with a sharp knife. Pour 5 cups of the beer and 3 cups of the water into a large bowl and stir in 4½ tbsp/80 g salt until the salt has completely dissolved. Add the lemon zest and peppercorns. Submerge the ham hocks in the brine, making sure they are completely covered. Cover with plastic wrap and refrigerate for at least 2 hours, or preferably overnight.

Preheat the oven to 350°F. Remove the ham hocks from the brine and discard the brine. Stir the honey and mustard together and rub it all over the ham hocks.

Place the onions, carrots, and celery in a large roasting dish and top with the ham hocks. Pour in 1 cup water and the remaining 1 cup beer. Cover with a layer of parchment, followed by a layer of foil. Bake for 3½ to 4 hours, basting the meat regularly with the juices and turning the hocks around from time to time. When done, the meat should be falling off the bone. For the last 30 minutes of the cooking time, remove the foil.

Meanwhile bring 2 cups water to a boil. Add the lentils, turn the heat to medium-low, and simmer until tender, about 20 minutes. Drain and toss the lentils with the parsley, lemon juice, and a pinch of salt.

Serve by piling the lentils on a platter with the shredded ham, carrots, and onions; pouring over some of the roasting juices.

Une petite astuce—tip If you're cooking four smaller ham hocks (each weighing roughly 1¼ lb/600 g), they will need 2½ to 3 hours in the oven. If you can only get salted ham hocks, rinse them in cold water before adding to the beer marinade, and leave out the salt.

Chaussons au jambon et légumes

HAM AND VEGETABLE PASTRY PUFFS

Maison Naegel is an iconic bakery in Strasbourg. I was lucky enough to get a behind-the-scenes tour to witness how they make their legendary *kugelhopf* (see my recipes on pages 254 and 258), but they are also famous for their *tourte*, a pie filled with a béchamel sauce, ham, and mushrooms. With some tasty leftovers from my Beer-Braised Ham Hock (page 241) burning a hole in my fridge, it was only a matter of putting two and two together to arrive at this glorious pastry puff. You can adjust or replace the filling to your liking.

Serves 4

Preparation time: 10 minutes
Cooking time: 45 minutes

18 oz/500 g puff pastry, at room temperature

9 oz/250 g ham, minced

3½ oz/100 g mature Comté or other strongly flavored cheese, cut into ½-inch chunks

1 boiled potato, chopped into ½-inch chunks

2 cooked carrots, chopped into ½-inch chunks

2 green onions, chopped into ½-inch pieces

1 egg

2 tbsp milk

Béchamel Sauce (page 276) for dipping

Preheat the oven to 400°F. Line a baking sheet with parchment. Roll out the puff pastry between two sheets of parchment to a thickness of ⅛ inch. Use a dessert plate (about 6½ inches in diameter) to cut out four pastry rounds.

In a small bowl, mix together the ham, Comté, potato, carrots, and green onions. Divide the filling between the pastry rounds, placing the mixture on one side of the circle. Be careful not to overfill and to leave at least ½ inch around the edge.

Whisk together the egg and milk to make an egg wash. Brush egg wash all around the edges of the pastry, then fold over the pastry so you have a half-moon shape. Use a fork or your finger to press down the pastry around the edge to seal. Prick the top with a fork and brush with egg wash. You can use the leftover pastry to cut out decorations to stick on.

Transfer the pastries to a baking sheet and bake for 30 minutes, until the bases are golden brown. Remove from the oven and transfer to a wire rack to cool. Serve warm or cold, with béchamel sauce for dipping.

Une petite astuce—tip Use any leftover cooked meat, poached fish, or vegetables—leeks, cheese, and potatoes make for a good combination.

Faire en avance—get ahead Chaussons can be assembled in advance and frozen for a couple of months in an airtight container (don't brush with egg wash before freezing). Add a few minutes to the baking time.

Mikaël Rochel, beef producer at Ferme des Fougères

Baeckehoffe

BAKER'S STEW

This dish is a wonder; you toss everything into a pot and leave it to simmer away. The story goes that on laundry day, wives would send their husbands and children off to work and school in the morning with the uncooked dish to drop off at the baker's. The baker would pop it into the cooler part of the oven, where it would slowly cook until being picked up by either the husband or the children on their way home. The lid of the dish would be sealed to keep out any fingers, so nothing got nibbled before it hit the dinner table.

Serves 6

Preparation time: 15 minutes
Resting time: overnight
(or 24 to 48 hours)
Cooking time: 3 to 4 hours

4 beef cheeks

4 slices of oxtail (about 1¾ lb/800 g)

4 thick slices of smoked bacon

3 cups Riesling wine

4 tomatoes

2 onions, quartered

3 carrots, peeled and halved
lengthwise

10 black peppercorns

2 cups water

2 large potatoes, peeled and
cut into thin slices

1 small butternut squash or pumpkin,
peeled and cut into thin slices

Pinch of salt

Place the beef cheeks, oxtail, bacon, and wine in a large container, making sure the meat is fully submerged. Cover with a lid or plastic wrap and marinate in the refrigerator overnight (or for a day or two).

When ready to cook, preheat the oven to 325°F.

Bring a small saucepan of water to a boil. Cut an X in the base of each tomato. Plunge the tomatoes into the boiling water for 30 seconds, remove, and, when cool enough to handle, peel.

Put the marinated meat, onions, carrots, tomatoes, and peppercorns in a large Dutch oven. Pour in the water and marinade. Try to create an even surface with no big gaps; this will make it easier to top with the slices of potato and butternut squash.

Neatly and tightly line up alternating rounds of potato and squash around the edge of the pot. The layers should begin to look like petals on a flower (see photographs, opposite). Lay the remaining slices over the top to cover the stew. Sprinkle with the salt.

Place a sheet of parchment on top, followed by the lid. Bake for 3 to 4 hours, until tender. Remove the lid and parchment, raise the heat to 450°F and broil for 5 to 10 minutes to crisp the potatoes and squash. Serve immediately.

In the Vosges mountains

Soupe au jambonneau et légumes

HAM HOCK AND VEGETABLE SOUP

The backbone of regional French cooking is its resourceful use of ingredients; celebrating lesser cuts, using every single part of the animal, and making a little go a long way. This soup is a celebration of leftovers, but that's not to say it isn't worthy of making from scratch.

Serves 4 to 6

Preparation time: 30 minutes
Cooking time: 30 minutes

1 cup/200 g pearl barley, farro, or spelt berries, rinsed

1 tbsp butter

2 carrots, peeled and chopped into ½-inch chunks

2 celery sticks, chopped into ½-inch chunks

1 onion, finely chopped

4 green onions, trimmed, green and white parts separated, finely chopped

2 tbsp grainy mustard

6 cups chicken stock

9 oz/250 g cooked lean ham hock, cut into small chunks

Salt and freshly ground black pepper

1 pear, cut into matchsticks

1 tbsp cider vinegar

Bring 2 cups water to a boil. Add the barley and boil for about 15 minutes, until tender. Drain. (Adjust cooking time as necessary if using farro or spelt berries.)

Melt the butter in a large saucepan over medium heat and add the carrots, celery, onion, and the green parts of the green onions. Cook for about 10 minutes, until tender but not golden, then stir in the mustard.

Add the stock, followed by the ham and cooked barley. Bring to a simmer over medium heat. Season with salt and pepper, and divide between serving bowls. Garnish with the white pieces of the green onions.

Place the pear in a small dish and pour the cider vinegar over it (do this just before serving the soup). Serve the pickled pear on the side, for adding to the soup.

Une petite astuce—tip If making this from scratch, boil a ham hock in a large pan of salted water with a carrot, onion, celery stick, a few peppercorns, and a couple of bay leaves. Simmer for about 3 hours, until the meat is soft and the broth is tasty. Then follow the recipe as directed.

Faire en avance—get ahead This soup will keep in a covered container, refrigerated, for up to 2 days.

Choux farcis sans saucisse

VEGETARIAN CABBAGE ROLLS

The French are blessed with some of the finest freshly grown produce. Despite this abundance, most dishes on the French menu will find a way of sneaking in a little something meaty, whether a sprinkling of lardons in a salad or a bit of sausage meat tucked into a tomato. Cabbage leaves make perfect flexible cases for holding flavorful stuffing ingredients, so here is my meat-free version—a great vegetarian dish.

Serves 4

Preparation time: 30 minutes
Cooking time: 55 minutes

1 savoy cabbage

4 tbsp olive oil, plus extra for drizzling

1 red onion, finely sliced

2 cloves of garlic, crushed

6 large sage leaves

Salt

⅓ cup/50 g seedless raisins

⅔ cup/100 g cooked and peeled chestnuts, roughly chopped

1 apple, cored and roughly cubed

1 sweet potato, baked in its skin

2 tbsp red wine vinegar

Zest of 1 lemon

3½ oz/100 g Munster cheese or chèvre, broken into chunks

Freshly ground black pepper

Peel away the tough leaves of the cabbage and cut out the tough inner core. Bring a large pot of water to a boil. Place the cabbage into the water and cook for 5 to 10 minutes, until soft but intact. Drain and let cool. Peel off about ten loose outer leaves and set aside. Finely chop the tighter part of the head.

Preheat the oven to 350°F. Heat the oil in a large frying pan over medium heat. Add the onion and garlic. Chop five of the sage leaves, add these, and season with salt. Cook for 5 minutes, until soft. Add the chopped cabbage and cook for 3 minutes more.

Add the raisins, chestnuts, apple, sweet potato, vinegar, and 2 tbsp water. Remove from the heat, and stir in the lemon zest and cheese. Season with salt and pepper.

Take two 20-inch lengths of butcher's string and form a cross in the base of a deep bowl, with the ends draped over the side. Place a couple of cabbage leaves on top of the string, overlapping them to create a nest for the filling. Spoon all the filling into the center of the leaves, then layer more leaves around the edges to overlap the bottom leaves, tucking them in and around the sides and covering the top of the filling.

Tie the strings together tightly on top in a neat bow, with the remaining sage leaf tucked underneath. Place the cabbage parcel on a baking sheet lined with parchment, sprinkle with a little salt, and drizzle with oil. Bake for 30 minutes.

Serve by cutting into wedges at the table.

Kugelhopf

KUGELHOPF

I was a woman on a mission when I visited Alsace. I had heard a lot about the famous *kugelhopf* and was in search of the ultimate version. I taste-tested the classic ones speckled with raisins, others accessorized with *tagada* (strawberry-flavored sweets), some studded with chocolate, and plenty of savory ones spiked with bacon. During my extensive *kugelhopf* research, I discovered that the best ones were very light and moist and made with the juiciest of raisins.

Kugelhopfs are typically baked in a ring-shaped mold called a *kugelhopf*, but if you don't have one, a loaf pan works well, too. The traditional Alsatian version is very similar to a brioche, made with yeast and enriched with butter and egg. My version is a little less buttery than its brioche cousin, but it's just as delicious. I've opted for lovely soft prunes to stud mine, but you can easily make the classic version with raisins or any other dried fruit you may have at home. See a photograph of the finished cake on page 256.

Serves 8

Preparation time: 45 minutes

Resting time: 6 hours, or preferably overnight

Cooking time: 30 minutes

Equipment: an 8-inch kugelhopf *mold or Pullman loaf pan*

1⅔ cups/300 g bread flour

3 tbsp sugar

1 tsp salt

1½ tsp instant yeast

2 eggs

½ cup milk, plus 2 tbsp

5 tbsp/70 g butter, cut into small cubes and softened, plus 1 tbsp for greasing

8 to 10 blanched almonds, for decoration (optional)

½ cup/70 g pitted soft prunes

In the bowl of a food processor fitted with the dough hook, combine the flour, sugar, salt, and yeast. Beat one of the eggs. Make a well in the middle of the flour and pour in the ½ cup milk and beaten egg. Mix on medium speed for 6 to 8 minutes, until the dough is soft, smooth, and elastic.

Add the butter, bit by bit, and continue to mix for about 5 minutes, until the butter is thoroughly incorporated. Scrape the bowl with a spatula to ensure all the butter is mixed in.

Once a dough has formed (it will be sticky), transfer it to a large clean bowl. Cover with plastic wrap and refrigerate until it has doubled in size (ideally overnight).

Grease the *kugelhopf* mold with the remaining 1 tbsp butter. If using a loaf pan, line it with parchment but do not grease it. Place an almond (if using) in each groove of the mold; if using a loaf pan, just scatter the almonds loosely in the bottom of the pan.

Lightly knead the prunes into the dough, keeping the kneading to a minimum.

Whisk the remaining egg and 2 tbsp milk together to make an egg wash. Shape the dough into a ball and poke a hole through the middle. Tuck it neatly into the mold, making sure the middle of the mold is peeking through the dough. Brush the dough with egg wash. If using a loaf pan, shape the dough into a sausage shape the length of the pan. Turn the dough into the pan and brush with egg wash. Cover with a clean damp tea towel or plastic wrap and leave somewhere warm until the dough has doubled in size.

Preheat the oven to 400°F. Brush the dough with more egg wash and bake for 30 minutes, or until a skewer inserted into the middle comes out clean. If the top is browning too quickly, cover loosely with foil.

Remove from the oven and cool for 10 minutes before turning out onto a wire rack to cool completely. The kugelhopf will keep, tightly wrapped, at room temperature, for up to 1 week.

Une petite astuce—tip If using dried prunes, cut them into ½-inch chunks and soak them in 3 tbsp Cognac, rum, or brandy overnight, or for at least the same amount of time the dough needs to rise in the fridge. It's important to leave the fruit plenty of time to soak up the alcohol as this will make it juicy. If you prefer not to use alcohol, freshly squeezed orange juice will work just as well. Drain the prunes of excess liquid before adding to the dough.

Kugelhopf marbré au fromage et aux épinards

SPINACH-CHEESE KUGELHOPF

After buying some traditional ceramic *kugelhopf* molds in Strasbourg (I was lucky enough to have bought two as I almost immediately broke one!), I went a little *kugelhopf* crazy. My bake-a-thon consisted of testing out an array of options, both sweet (see page 254) and savory. This recipe uses ingredients that produce a fun pattern in the bread. Spinach lends itself well as a natural dye, giving the dough a deep green color, as well as keeping the bread deliciously moist. The bread can be served on its own or cut into slices and eaten with cold meats and cheese. See the photographs on page 257 showing how to make this *kugelhopf*.

Serves 8

Preparation time: 45 minutes

Resting time: 6 hours, or preferably overnight

Cooking time: 45 minutes

Equipment: an 8-inch kugelhopf *mold or a Pullman loaf pan*

For the normal dough

1¼ cups/150 g bread flour

1 tsp sugar

½ tsp salt

1 tsp instant yeast

3 tbsp milk

1 egg, beaten

2½ tbsp/35 g unsalted butter, cut into small cubes and softened

2½ oz/75 g finely grated mature Comté, Cheddar, or other strongly flavored hard cheese

To make the normal dough: In the bowl of a food processor fitted with the dough hook, mix together the flour, sugar, salt, and yeast. Make a well in the middle of the flour and pour in the milk and egg. Mix on medium speed for 6 to 8 minutes, until the dough is soft, smooth, and elastic.

Add the softened butter, bit by bit, and continue to mix for about 5 minutes, until the butter is thoroughly incorporated. Add the grated Comté and continue to mix. Scrape the sides of the bowl with a spatula to ensure all the butter is mixed in.

Once a dough has formed (it will be sticky), transfer it to a large clean bowl. Cover with plastic wrap and refrigerate until it has doubled in size (ideally overnight).

To make the spinach dough: Cook the spinach in a pot of boiling water for 10 to 15 minutes. Drain and, when cool enough to handle, squeeze out the excess water. Stir the butter into the spinach and let cool. Add the salt and nutmeg and season with pepper (see Tip).

Mix together the flour and yeast in a large bowl. Add the spinach mixture and knead until you have a smooth ball of dough (it may be a little sticky). Place in a bowl, cover with plastic wrap, and refrigerate along with the plain dough.

For the spinach dough

14 oz/400 g frozen spinach

2½ tbsp unsalted butter, softened

1 tsp salt

½ tsp freshly grated nutmeg

Coarsely ground black pepper

1¼ cups/150 g bread flour

1 tsp instant yeast

1 egg

2 tbsp milk

1 tbsp unsalted butter

Handful of pine nuts

Lightly dust a work surface with flour. Whisk together the egg and milk to make an egg wash. Roll out the normal dough to form a rectangle roughly 8 by 12 inches, with the long side facing you. Brush egg wash over the dough. Do the same with the spinach dough and lay it on top of the normal dough. Fold the bottom edge to the middle, and fold over the top half to meet it. Brush with egg wash and then fold the bottom half over the top half. Brush the ends with egg wash and stick them together to form a ring. (If you're using a loaf pan, skip this last step.)

Grease the mold with the butter. If using a loaf pan, line it with parchment but do not grease it. Scatter the base with the pine nuts. Place the ring of dough in the mold and brush with egg wash. If using a loaf pan, shape the dough into a sausage shape the length of the pan. Turn the dough into the pan and brush with egg wash. Cover with a clean, damp tea towel or plastic wrap and leave somewhere warm to rise until the dough has doubled in size.

Preheat the oven to 400°F. Brush the *kugelhopf* with the remaining egg wash and bake for 30 minutes, or until a skewer inserted into the middle comes out clean. If the top browns too quickly as it cooks, cover loosely with foil.

Remove from the oven and let cool for 10 minutes before turning out onto a wire rack to cool completely. The kugelhopf will keep, tightly wrapped, at room temperature, for up to 1 week.

Une petite astuce—tip Overseason the spinach with nutmeg and pepper, as the flour will dilute the flavor.

Tarte au fromage blanc

CREAMY CHEESE TART

When asked to imagine a cheesecake, almost everyone thinks of the famous New York incarnation. Well, Alsace is the home of the French cheesecake, and it is by no sheer coincidence that it also happens to produce the most unctuous and creamy fromage blanc in France. Contrary to the popular belief that French food is very rich, Alsatian cheesecake is remarkably light and airy, getting its lift from a billowy meringue base.

Serves 6 to 8

Preparation time: 30 minutes
Resting time: 1½ hours
Cooking time: 1¼ hours
Equipment: a 9½-inch springform cake pan

½ recipe Sweet Pastry Dough (page 275)

2 egg yolks, plus 7 egg whites

Zest and juice of 1 lemon

1 tsp vanilla extract

1½ cups/150 g confectioners' sugar

⅓ cup/40 g cornstarch

6 tbsp/50 g powdered milk

1¼ cups/300 g fromage blanc, Greek yogurt, or quark

Grease the springform pan and line it with parchment. Wrap a double layer of foil around the outside.

Using your hands, squash the pastry dough into a ball. Transfer it to the prepared cake pan and use the palm of your hand and a spatula to carefully flatten it out to evenly cover the base of the pan. Prick the pastry base with a fork and refrigerate for 30 minutes. Preheat the oven to 350°F.

Bake the pastry for 15 minutes, until golden, then remove from the oven and let cool. Meanwhile, whisk the egg yolks with the lemon zest, vanilla, and half of the confectioners' sugar until thick and creamy. Beat in the cornstarch and powdered milk, followed by the fromage blanc.

In a separate glass or metal bowl, begin to whisk the egg whites with 2 to 3 tbsp confectioners' sugar. When the whites are foamy, add the lemon juice and the rest of the confectioners' sugar, and whisk until soft peaks form. Beat one-third of the egg whites into the fromage blanc mixture until smooth. Gently fold in the rest of the egg whites.

Place the cake pan in a large, deep roasting pan and fill the cake pan with the egg white mixture. Smooth with a spatula. Pour water into the roasting pan to a depth of about ¾ inch. Carefully place in the oven and immediately lower the temperature to 250°F. Bake for 1 hour, turn off the heat, and leave in the oven for another hour with the door open. Run a sharp knife around the inside edges of the cake pan before unmolding the cheesecake. Slice and serve.

Berawecka

SPICED FRUIT AND NUT LOAF

In my mind, this is the Alsatian version of the British Christmas cake; a dense loaf packed with dried fruit and nuts galore and with a hint of spice and rum. When you cut a slice from the loaf, the juicy fruit-and-nut filling is revealed. I love to eat a thin slice, toasted and slathered with butter, and it works equally well as part of a cheese platter.

Makes 2 loaves

Preparation time: 20 to 25 minutes
Soaking time: 10 to 48 hours
Resting time: 3 to 4 hours
Cooking time: 30 to 35 minutes

½ cup/100 g finely chopped candied orange

½ cup/100 g dried figs, roughly chopped

½ cup/100 g dried apricots, blueberries, or cranberries

½ cup/100 g raisins

2 tsp ground cinnamon

1 tsp ground ginger

6½ tbsp rum

Zest of 1 lemon

Zest and juice of 1 orange

1¼ cups/150 g bread flour

1¼ cups/150 g whole wheat flour

2 tsp instant yeast

1 tsp salt

¾ cup water

5½ oz/150 g firm pears, cored and grated

⅔ cup/100 g walnuts, roughly chopped

1 egg

2 tbsp milk

In a medium bowl, mix the candied orange, figs, apricots, raisins, cinnamon, ginger, rum, lemon zest, and orange zest and juice and soak at least overnight, or up to 2 days.

In a large bowl, sift together the bread flour, whole wheat flour, yeast, and salt. Make a well in the center of the flour and pour in the water. Draw in the flour from the edges of the bowl and knead by hand for 10 to 15 minutes. (If the dough feels sticky, sprinkle it with a little flour.) Cover with a clean, damp tea towel or plastic wrap and leave in a warm place for 2 to 3 hours.

Add the grated pear and walnuts to the soaked fruit. Mix together and drain off any excess liquid. Turn the dough out on a work surface and cut into three equal parts. Return one part to the bowl and combine it with the fruit mixture, kneading it together with your fingers. Set aside.

The two remaining pieces of dough will be used to make the outside of the loaves. Roll each piece into a rectangle (8 by 12 inches and 1/16 inch thick). Whisk together the egg and milk to make an egg wash and brush over the dough. Place half of the fruit mixture in the middle of one sheet of dough and pat it down to form an even layer, leaving enough dough on each side to cover the filling. Fold in the sides and place on a baking sheet, with the folds underneath. Repeat for the second loaf.

Brush the loaves with egg wash and prick all over with a fork. Leave in a warm place for 30 minutes. Preheat the oven to 400°F. Apply a second coat of egg wash and bake for 30 to 35 minutes. The loaves should have a rich brown color. Remove from the oven and let cool on a wire rack for at least 5 minutes before slicing. This will keep, tightly wrapped, at room temperature, for up to 1 week.

Boules de neige à la noix de coco

COCONUT SNOWBALLS

When I visited Alsace just before Christmas, a veil of fresh snow dusted the countryside, perfect for getting that festive feeling going. These little coconut snowballs lie somewhere between a macaroon and a meringue; snow-white and puffy, like perfect little *boules de neige*.

Makes 20 to 24 cookies

Preparation time: 10 minutes using an electric whisk or food processor, or 30 minutes by hand

Cooking time: 1 hour

2 egg whites

2 drops of lemon juice

6 tbsp/80 g sugar

Pinch of salt

1¾ cups/150 g coconut flakes

Preheat the oven to 200°F. Line a baking sheet with parchment.

Whisk the egg whites until white and slightly thickened. Whisk in the lemon juice. Gradually sprinkle in the sugar and salt, while whisking, until stiff peaks form. Fold in the coconut.

Using two teaspoons, form small balls of the mixture and carefully drop them onto the lined baking sheet. Place the sheet in the oven and use a wooden spoon to wedge open the oven door slightly. Bake for 1 hour, or until the snowballs are dry on the outside but still slightly moist in the middle. When cooked, they should slide off the paper easily.

Remove the cookies from the parchment and cool completely on a wire rack. These will keep in an airtight container for up to 3 weeks.

Une petite astuce—tip Make sure the egg whites are opaque and have thickened slightly before incorporating the sugar; otherwise they won't form stiff peaks.

Schwowebredele

SPICED ALMOND COOKIES

Nutty, crunchy, and fragrant with plenty of sweet spices, these cookies are definitely among my favorites, having sampled many different types of *bredele* (Christmas cookies).

Makes about 40 cookies

Preparation time: 25 minutes
Resting time: 2 hours, or overnight
Cooking time: 10 minutes
Equipment: a selection of cookie cutters

2 cups/250 g all-purpose flour

2 tsp baking powder

1¼ cups/125 g ground almonds

Zest and juice of 1 lemon

Zest of 1 orange

½ cup/125 g finely chopped candied orange, or ⅓ cup/100 g chunky marmalade, strained and orange pieces chopped

2 tbsp ground cinnamon

½ cup plus 1 tbsp/125 g butter

¾ cup/150 g packed dark brown sugar

1 egg, beaten

In a large bowl, mix together the flour, baking powder, ground almonds, lemon zest, orange zest, candied orange, and cinnamon. In a separate bowl, beat together the butter and brown sugar until fluffy. Add the egg, followed by the lemon juice. Stir the dry ingredients into the wet ingredients and mix until fully incorporated. Refrigerate for 2 hours, or, ideally, overnight.

Line a baking sheet with parchment. Divide the dough in half and roll between two sheets of parchment to a thickness of ¹⁄₁₆ inch.

Using the cutters, cut out the cookies and place them on the sheet, leaving a finger-width space between them. Repeat until all the dough is used (you can reroll any cut-offs). Refrigerate the cutouts. Preheat the oven to 350°F.

Bake for 10 minutes, or until the edges of the cookies are browned. They will be slightly soft when they come out of the oven. Let cool on a wire rack. The cookies will keep in an airtight container for up to 1 month.

Une petite astuce—tip If your dough is too soft to handle at any point when rolling, freeze it briefly.

Faire en avance—get ahead The dough freezes well. Remove from the freezer about 1 hour before rolling out.

Baking fingerle with Madame Geisert

Fingerle

FINGER COOKIES

Baking cookies for Christmas is a longstanding tradition in the Alsace region, with many different variations all captured under the title *bredele*. Madame Geisert, who has been baking cookies for longer than she can remember, and now bakes them with her grandchildren, gave me a special lesson in *fingerle*. Traditionally, they are simply rolled in plain sugar to give them a crystal crust, but I like to roll mine in flavored sugars to give them an extra twist.

Makes about 60 cookies
Preparation time: 20 minutes
Resting time: 1 hour
Cooking time: 10 minutes

½ cup plus 1 tbsp/125 g unsalted butter

1 cup/200 g sugar

1 tsp vanilla extract

1 egg

2 cups/250 g all-purpose flour

1½ tsp baking powder

Pinch of salt

¼ tsp ground cinnamon

½ tsp lemon zest

Using a handheld or stand mixer, beat the butter, ¾ cup/125 g of the sugar, and the vanilla until pale and fluffy. Add the egg and combine. Add the flour, baking powder, and salt and use a pastry cutter or a fork to chop up the mixture until it is crumbly. Then, using your hands, bring it together to form a ball. Wrap the dough in plastic wrap and refrigerate for 1 hour.

Preheat the oven to 350°F. Line a baking sheet with parchment. Pour one-third of the remaining sugar onto a plate. Mix another third of the sugar with the cinnamon and spread on another plate. Repeat with the lemon zest and remaining sugar.

Split the dough into three equal parts. Take one piece and roll it between your palms or on a work surface to make a long sausage, about ½ inch thick. Cut the sausage into small finger lengths. Roll and lightly press each piece into one of the sugars. Repeat for the remaining pieces of dough, rolling in one of the different sugars, and place on the baking sheet.

Bake for 10 minutes; the cookies should remain pale. Remove from the oven and let cool on a wire rack. The cookies will keep in an airtight container for up to 2 weeks.

Une petite astuce—tip If the dough melts in your hands while you're making the *fingerle*, rinse your hands under cold water to cool them down, and make sure you dry them thoroughly.

Faire en avance—get ahead Make your lemon sugar a couple of days in advance and keep it in an airtight container; the flavor will be stronger.

Notes

A note on equipment

While my apartment doesn't boast the largest kitchen, I do have a decent amount of equipment I can't live without.

When it comes to baking, precision is important and **digital scales** are a must for recipes such as Choux Pastry and Shortcrust Pastry (both on page 274). A set of **measuring spoons** is very useful for measuring yeast (see the brioche and *kugelhopf* on pages 218 and 254).

I use a lot of **piping bags**, disposable or otherwise. These give a neat and more professional look to even the simplest of things, and allow you to be a little more accurate with the details (for example, the chocolate eggs on page 215).

Muslin or **cheesecloth** is excellent for straining broths (like the *tourin* on page 70) and poaching, and can be easily machine-washed for reuse.

Microplane zesters make easy work of zesting lemons and oranges, and I always have a **peeler** on hand for vegetable ribbons as well as peeling vegetables. A small Japanese **mandoline** slices quickly and precisely for perfect vegetable rounds (for example in the vegetable *tian* on page 166) and easy onion-slicing in an instant.

Digital thermometers come in handy for making caramel (see page 48) and tempering chocolate (as for the chestnut truffles on page 169).

To sterilize jars (for the marinated vegetables on page 154 and the Espelette pepper jelly on page 127), either run them through the hottest cycle in the dishwasher or wash in soapy water, rinse well, and then place, open, in a 275°F oven for 15 to 20 minutes.

A note on ingredients

Butter I use unsalted butter unless otherwise stated. See also the note on French dairy produce, opposite.

Citrus fruit All citrus fruit, especially where the zest is used, should be unwaxed and preferably organic.

Eggs Medium, ideally organic, eggs are used in all the recipes unless specified otherwise.

Egg whites These can be stored in an airtight container in the refrigerator for up to 4 weeks and frozen for up to 3 months. The average weight of an egg is 2 oz/55 g, with the white weighing just over ¾ oz/25 g. So if a recipe calls for 1 egg white and you have stored them together, simply measure out the white to approximately ¾ oz/25 g using a digital scale.

Fish Always buy responsibly sourced fish and experiment with more sustainable varieties.

Gelatin My recipes use sheet gelatin. Gelatin sheets require soaking in cold water and then squeezing to remove excess moisture before adding to warm liquid.

Salt I use sea salt such as Maldon or *fleur de sel* for seasoning my dishes. The taste is milder than average table salt and the small investment makes a world of difference.

Sugar Superfine sugar is used in my recipes unless otherwise stated.

Vanilla pods Plump Bourbon or Tahiti vanilla pods are ideal for cooking. Once you have removed the seeds, dry the pods out in a low oven; you can add them to a jar of sugar to make vanilla sugar.

Yeast I use instant or fast-acting dried yeast, which can be added directly to the dry ingredients in your baking without the need to activate separately.

Some notes on French dairy produce

Living in France and having access to the best *fromageries* has certainly had an impact on how I cook. France is highly regional in its dairy consumption; while butter and cream features heavily in Normandy and Brittany, olive oil is favored in the south.

If you are vegetarian, be sure to check if your cheese contains animal rennet.

Fromage blanc Thick, creamy fromage blanc generally has a higher fat content than fromage frais; quark is a good substitute if the former is not available.

Crème fraîche The thick French version of sour cream, available in most supermarkets and always to be found in my fridge.

Buttermilk—*Lait ribot* Buttermilk is a by-product of butter-making and it is widely used in Brittany and Normandy. Using buttermilk in cooking has many benefits, from giving pancakes a light and fluffy texture to breaking down the proteins in meat, tenderizing it. (See the buttermilk lamb on page 30.)

Basics
Choux Pastry Dough

½ cup water • ½ cup milk • ½ cup/100 g butter, cut into cubes • Pinch of salt • 1 tsp sugar • 1⅓ cups/170 g bread flour, sifted • 4 eggs

Pour the water and milk into a small saucepan and add the butter, salt, and sugar. Place the pan over high heat until the butter is melted and the liquid is simmering around the edges. Turn the heat to low, add all of the flour, and beat hard. Continue beating until you have a smooth ball that pulls away from the sides of the pan without sticking.

Remove the pan from the heat and continue to beat until the dough is cool enough to touch. Mix in the eggs, one at a time; the batter will be lumpy when you first add them, but beating continuously will smooth it out. Once all the eggs are incorporated and the mixture is smooth, it is ready to be scraped into a piping bag.

Les petites astuces—tips Make sure the liquid is simmering around the edges before you add the flour. If the mixture isn't hot enough, the starch in the flour will not be activated and the batter will not thicken.

Make sure to beat over low heat. At first it will be a lumpy mashed-potato consistency and then a big smooth lump.

Use medium-size eggs. If the eggs are too big, it will make your batter too runny. If you want to be super-precise, 1 egg without its shell should weigh 1¾ oz/50 g.

Incorporate the eggs while the mixture is still warm but not boiling hot. If it's too cold, the eggs will be harder to incorporate, and the batter may be runnier.

Shortcrust Pastry Dough

6 tbsp/90 g butter, softened • ½ cup/45 g confectioners' sugar • Pinch of salt • 2 egg yolks • 1 cup plus 1 tbsp/135 g all-purpose flour

Using a wooden spoon, beat together the butter, confectioners' sugar, and salt until soft and creamy. Mix in the egg yolks to make a smooth paste. Add the flour and use a pastry cutter or fork to chop up the mixture until it has a sandy texture. Use your hand to gently shape the dough into a ball and then wrap in plastic wrap and refrigerate for at least 1 hour.

Sweet Pastry Dough

½ cup plus 1 tbsp/120 g butter, softened • ½ cup plus 2 tbsp/60 g confectioners' sugar • Pinch of salt •
2 egg yolks • 1½ cups/180 g all-purpose flour

Using a wooden spoon, beat together the butter, confectioners' sugar, and salt until soft and creamy. Mix in the egg yolks to make a smooth paste, then add the flour. Use a pastry cutter or a fork to chop up the mixture until it has a sandy texture, making sure you incorporate all the flour into the butter. Squash the dough into a ball with your hands, wrap in plastic wrap, and refrigerate for at least 1 hour.

Flatbread Dough

1¼ cups/150 g bread flour • ¾ cup/100 g whole wheat bread flour • 1 tsp instant yeast • ½ tsp salt •
1 tsp sugar • ½ cup warm water • 1 tbsp olive oil • 4 shallots, halved and finely sliced •
2 tbsp finely chopped herbs (a mixture of parsley, dill, and chives works well)

Mix together the bread flour, whole wheat flour, yeast, salt, and sugar in a large bowl. Add the water and oil and bring together with your hands. Knead intensively for 10 minutes, or, ideally, use the dough hook on a stand mixer. Add the shallots and herbs and bring the mixture together to form a smooth dough. Place the dough in a bowl and cover with a clean damp tea towel or plastic wrap and leave in a warm place for 1 hour.

Pizza Dough

2 cups/250 g all-purpose flour • 1 tsp salt • 2 tsp instant yeast • ¼ cup olive oil • ⅝ cup warm water

Mix together the flour, salt, and yeast in a large bowl. Make a well in the center and pour in the oil and water. Mix together to incorporate and then turn out onto a floured surface and knead until the dough is smooth and elastic, about 10 minutes. Return the dough to the bowl and rest at room temperature for 30 minutes. (The dough can be made up to 1 day in advance. Keep it refrigerated in a bowl, covered in plastic wrap.)

Béchamel Sauce

2 tbsp butter • ¼ cup/30 g all-purpose flour • 2 cups lukewarm milk • ¼ onion, peeled • 1 clove •
1 bay leaf • Pinch of grated nutmeg • Salt and white pepper

Melt the butter in a large saucepan over medium heat. Add the flour and beat hard with a wooden spoon to a smooth paste. Remove from the heat and gradually add ½ cup of the milk, beating all the time. Switch to a whisk and add the rest of the milk a little at a time, whisking constantly.

Place the pan back over medium heat; add the onion, clove, and bay leaf; and simmer for 10 minutes. Whisk frequently to prevent it from sticking. (If the sauce becomes too thick, whisk in a little more milk; it should be like thick custard.) Remove and discard the onion, clove, and bay leaf, then add the nutmeg and season with salt and pepper. Pour the béchamel into a bowl and cover with a layer of plastic wrap touching the surface (to prevent a skin from forming). Refrigerate until cool. Use the béchamel sauce on the day you make it; it will not keep.

Mayonnaise

2 egg yolks • 1 clove of garlic, crushed • 1¼ cups sunflower oil • Lemon juice, to taste • Sea salt

Place the egg yolks and garlic in a large glass or metal bowl set on a damp tea towel (to stop the bowl from slipping). Whisk the egg yolks a little, then add the sunflower oil drop by drop until the eggs begin to thicken and become pale in color. Continue drizzling in the oil until you have achieved the consistency you like. Add lemon juice and season with sea salt. Use the mayonnaise on the day you make it; it will not keep.

Une petite astuce—tip If you have a food processor, process the egg yolks and the garlic, then gradually add the oil until you achieve the desired consistency.

Praline

2 oz/50 g blanched skinless hazelnuts • 6 tbsp/75 g sugar • 2 tbsp water

Line a baking sheet with parchment. In a small sauté pan over medium heat, toast the hazelnuts until they are golden. Set aside. Put the sugar and water in the pan over low heat until the sugar dissolves. Increase the heat to high (resist the temptation to stir it). When the caramel begins to turn a dark golden brown, remove from the heat and quickly stir in the hazelnuts. Pour immediately onto the lined baking sheet and spread out evenly to cool. (The praline can be made up to this point 1 month ahead; store in an airtight container.) Once the caramel is cool and hard, pulse it to a fine powder in a food processor.

Index

Page numbers for photographs are in **bold**

G

Galette des rois 54, **55**

galettes: tomato and lentil mille-feuille 18, **19**

garlic: chicken in a pot with crispy garlic rice 72, **73**

Gâteau aux carottes et noix de coco **88**, 89

Gâteaux de la Dune du Pyla 94, **95**

Gelée de piment d'Espelette **126**, 127

ginger:

caramel, ginger, and raspberry lighthouses 46, **47**

Lillet, ginger, and lemon fizz 100, **101**

globe artichokes: ratatouille aperitif 154, **155**

goat cheese, strawberry, and cucumber mille-feuilles **158**, 159

grapefruit: sunshine salad **150**, 151

grapes: crispy duck and roasted Sauternes grape wraps 80, **81**

green bean bundles with herb lentil salad 210, **211**

H

haddock: new Lyonnais salad **188**, 189

ham:

beer-braised ham hock **240**, 241

green bean bundles with herb lentil salad 210, **211**

ham and zucchini ribbons with melon 105, **107**

ham hock and vegetable soup 250, **251**

ham and vegetable pastry puffs 242, **243**

white asparagus in blankets 66, **67**

Haricots savoyard avec lentilles aux herbes 210, **211**

hazelnut-crusted monkfish cheeks with a sunshine salad **150**, 151

herbs:

green bean bundles with herb lentil salad 210, **211**

herby salt crust–baked bream 16, **17**

vegetables stuffed with red rice and herbes de Provence 144, **145**

honey: nougat mousse 180, **181**

horseradish: Alsatian noodles **236**, 237

hot dogs: baby brioche hot dogs **194**, 195

Huîtres avec un bouillon Bordelais 58, **59**

Huîtres grillées en persillade 12, **13**

I

ice cream: sand dune ice-cream cakes 94, **95**

J

jam: cherry jam Lamingtons **107**, 108

Jambonneau à la bière **240**, 241

Joues de lotte de mer en croûte de noisette avec une salade **150**, 151

K

ketchup: bacon and Basque ketchup sandwich 125

kidneys: smoked sausage and kidney pie 202, **203**

king's cake 54, **55**

kiwis: crab and kiwi tartare **60**, 61

Knepfles à l'épeautre avec Munster et feuilles d'oignons 226, **227**

koftas: beef koftas with herby flatbreads 84, **85**

kohlrabi: roasted chicken parcels with kohlrabi slaw 38, **39**

Les kouignettes aux groseilles 42–3, **44–5**

Kugelhopf 254–5, **256**

Kugelhopf marbré au fromage et aux épinards **257**, 258–9

L

lamb: buttermilk lamb with toasted buckwheat and herb salad 30, **31**

Lamingtons: cherry jam Lamingtons **107**, 108

lardons: Alsatian noodles **236**, 237

lemons:

chard and preserved lemon blinis **146**, 147

Lillet, ginger, and lemon fizz 100, **101**

lentils:

green bean bundles with herb lentil salad 210, **211**

tomato and lentil mille-feuille 18, **19**

lettuces: Little Gems with mustard vinaigrette and Gruyère 105, **107**

Lillet, ginger, and lemon fizz 100, **101**

lima beans: pork and clams with cider and lima beans 120, **121**

little gems with mustard vinaigrette and Gruyère 105, **107**

lobster, fennel, and buttermilk soup 34, **35–7**

Lyonnais pizza 190, **191**

M

marzipan: date and marzipan rolls **107**, 109

mayonnaise 276

Acknowledgments

Writing a book—and certainly a cookbook—is not an easy feat. It is not a simple act of sitting down and typing away on the computer. This book started with me getting on a train, a plane, and other modes of transport to visit, meet, and learn new things about the different food traditions around France. The inspiration for these recipes would not have been possible without the help of the many people I met along the way (some of the pictured and written about in the book). To all the producers, bakers, cooks, farmers, and passionate food people (Michaela Spielvogel at Slow Food France), *un GRAND merci*!

Back in the kitchen it was my trusty two-ring gas hob, toy-size oven, and my friends who were there giving me feedback on the concoctions I created. Thanks for being great guinea pigs, guys!

Special thank-you to Lindsey Evans and the whole team at Penguin for being encouraging, supportive, and excited about my new adventures beyond my little Paris kitchen.

Cher John Hamilton, *merci beaucoup* for all your hard work and enthusiasm for this book. Your attention to detail has made it special.

Chère Lizzy Kremer, you're the best literary agent one could wish for. Your support and the team at David Higham has helped me to grow as a food writer.

Cher David Loftus, as always you make my food (and me) look beautiful, regardless of the weather or late night. And, BIG thank-you for putting up with my "love of speed" in the car.

Chère Nathalie Redard, thank you for searching the lengths and breadths of France to find the perfect plate, fork, or other prop paraphernalia. It has certainly paid off, because the dishes look fantastic!

Chère Frankie Unsworth, *merci mille fois* for traipsing in the rain and mud and getting lost in the French countryside with me. Your hard work has helped me make this book the best it can be. I couldn't have done it without you!

Chèrs my loving family and Robert Wiktorin. Thank you for being there and putting up with me no matter my mood.

Many thanks to all the people who helped out on the photo shoots around France: Marie Constantinesco, Amie Brennan, Sarah McLoughlin, Amélie Riberolle. Véronique Daudin at Ecolodge des Chartrons, Aurélien Crosato, Madame and Monsieur Constaninesco, Jean-Luc Colonna, Daniel Rozensztroch, Régis Godon, Elisabeth Simon, Marianne Ménard, Catherine Madani, Genevieve Goux, Anne Cardot, Hélène de Bettignie, Laurence Lagrange, Papier Tigre, Myriam Balay Devidal, Gabrielle Franck, Émilie Mazeaud, Nathalie and Christophe Hurtault, Marjorie Goaoc, Elodie Rambaud, Bachelier Antiquités.

And the shops and brands for lending us some beautiful props:

MERCI
www.merci-merci.com

BACHELIER ANTIQUITES
www.bachelier-antiquites.com

ASTIER DE VILLATTE
www.astierdevillatte.com

MEMENTO
www.facebook.com/MementoBrocante

ARTOCARPUS
www.facebook.com/galerieartocarpus

COPIRATES
lescopirates.fr

PIED DE POULE
www.pieddepoule.com

STAUB
www.staub.fr

LES GUIMARDS
www.lesguimards.com

MUD
www.mudaustralia.com

LE GARDE MANGER
www.facebook.com/pages/Le-Garde-Manger-Aligre-Paris-12%C3%A8me/106656756022428

LE PRÉ AUX CLAIRS
www.lepreauxclairs.com

LA COLLINE
www.facebook.com/pages/La-Colline/273845949372350

Merci beaucoup, à bientôt